The
CURTAIN
BOOK

The CURTAIN *BOOK*

A Sourcebook for
Distinctive Curtains, Drapes, and Shades
for Your Home

CAROLINE CLIFTON-MOGG AND MELANIE PAINE

Photography by Fritz von der Schulenburg

A Bulfinch Press Book
Little, Brown and Company
Boston New York Toronto London

First United States Paperback Edition 1995
Fourth printing, 1997

First published in Great Britain in 1988 by Mitchell Beazley,
an imprint of Reed Consumer Books Ltd

ISBN 0-8212-2194-9

Library of Congress Catalog Card Number 94-73296

Senior Executive Art Editor   **Jacqui Small**
Assistant Art Editor   **Larraine Lacey**

Executive Editor   **Robert Saxton**
Editor   **Margaret Crowther**

Production   **Ted Timberlake**
Illustrations   **Caroline Bays**

Archive pictures supplied by courtesy of
Raymond O'Shea, the O'Shea Galleries, London

Bulfinch Press is an imprint and trademark of
Little, Brown and Company (Inc.)

Published simultaneously in Canada by
Little, Brown & Company (Canada) Limited

PRINTED IN HONG KONG

CONTENTS

Introduction   7

INTRODUCTION

A curtain arrangement is often the most eye-catching aspect of a room – and the feature that gives most scope for creativity. Some windows are beautiful in themselves, and the art in such cases is to ensure that the "dressing" of fabric complements, rather than obscures, the "architectural" framework. Where the windows have no intrinsic merit, the options for curtaining are much wider.

The chief ingredient in any successful window composition is imagination. To some extent, there is a repertoire of basic forms – a vocabulary of design ideas from which professional designers tend to draw inspiration. Often, the most successful designs are those where a traditional idea is injected with a touch of originality – perhaps in the proportions, or in the detailing, or in the fabric choice.

Details can make all the difference. Notice, for example, in the room on the opposite page, how the narrow floral borders on the undercurtains frame and continue the slender lines of the candlestick. This is the kind of subtlety that makes for maximum effectiveness. Of course, what we notice first about this room is the match between curtains, furnishing fabrics and walls, illustrating another key principle – the importance of keeping the curtains in consonance with the rest of the room, to create a coherent mood. The window arrangement should never look as if it has been designed in isolation.

Curtain designs these days show a spirit of adventurousness that has seldom been equalled. Historic styles are being freely and imaginatively adapted; bed curtains are fashionable again; shades have lost their overtones of functionalism and have acquired a new excitement, whether used alone or as an underdressing to curtains. It is hoped that this book will promote as well as reflect the inventiveness to be found in the use of curtains, shades and drapes in today's most beautiful interiors.

BEGINNINGS

Textiles were used as decorative hangings in medieval Europe, but not in the form of window dressings. Windows in those days were small and narrow, for defensive reasons: they let out smoke and fumes but light was not a major priority. Usually, their only covering was a crude wooden shutter to provide security and protection from the elements. A covering of strong oiled or waxed paper was sometimes used, but its purpose was practical rather than ornamental: glazed windows in houses were rare, and remained so until well into the 16th century.

Only the nobility had enough wealth to make their homes comfortable. As they were always on the move, the items on which most money or skill was lavished were the portable hangings. Woven hangings were a necessity: hung against the damp, cold walls, they kept in the warmth, and across doorways in the cheerless halls they acted as barriers for drafts. Another vital use, which gained in importance over the years, was around the bed.

Hangings for both wall and bed were full of color, rich and bold, depicting scenes from legend and from daily life. As the Middle Ages progressed, designs became ever more sumptuous, often with rich embroidery. From the 12th century, fine silks were produced in Italy, at Lucca and soon at Venice; and by the 14th century, rich velvets were woven in centers such as Genoa, Florence and Milan. The simpler houses, where such hangings were out of the question, had plain linen or woollen materials, sometimes crudely painted.

As hangings became richer, furniture developed in tandem. The bed gained in importance: beginning as a simple wooden framework, crudely curtained, by the end of the 15th century it had carved posts, legs and headboard, and an ornate fabric canopy. The age of exuberance was dawning.

◁

WALL HANGINGS AND A BATHTUB DRESSED WITH MUSLIN CURTAINS RISING TO A CORONET HAVE AN UNMISTAKABLY MEDIEVAL FEEL IN THIS CASTLE BEDROOM.

▷

DOOR CURTAINS IN THE FORM OF TAPESTRIES AND HANGINGS WERE MUCH USED BETWEEN THE 13TH AND 16TH CENTURIES AS PRACTICAL AND DECORATIVE DRAFT EXCLUDERS.

△

A ROMANTICIZED VIEW OF MEDIEVAL FABRIC BED HANGINGS AND WINDOW DRESSINGS WAS FERVENTLY ADOPTED BY THE VICTORIANS.

TUDOR HANGINGS

In England, the Elizabethans, while showing sensitivity in poetry, painting and music, did not bring the same delicacy to their dress or furniture. Pieces in oak were heavy and crudely carved. However, the furnishings that accompanied them were rich and beautiful. Bright, exuberantly painted or embroidered cloths and jewel-colored tapestries covered the walls, engulfed the beds, and began to appear at windows.

The box-like beds became huge, with elaborate hangings. The bed of Henry VIII and Ann Boleyn measured 11 feet (3.3 meters) square. Elizabeth I had a bed with hangings of cloth woven with silver thread, trimmed with gold, silver lace and fringes, with a white satin ceiling – the whole confection painted with hundreds of flower sprigs.

This opulence was widely imitated on a lesser scale. Even simpler folk had hangings of wool and linen – often brightly painted to resemble tapestries. The grandest tapestries and hangings were still mainly woven in Europe, but there were now several weaving works in England, such as William Sheldon's famous works in Warwickshire.

From the later 16th century, window curtains became a more important part of room decoration – particularly in Europe. In England, such curtains were fairly basic, consisting, in all but the homes of the grandest courtiers, of a simple, fixed narrow strip of fabric. Curtains in pairs were uncommon. The large new windows sometimes had small panels of stained glass set into them as ornament.

The picture on the Continent was somewhat different. The Italians and French, style-setters even then, had far more elaborate curtains, made from rich brocades and velvets, in shades of orange, brown and dark green. Fairly narrow, and falling well short of the floor, they hung simply in pairs.

THE 17TH CENTURY

The 17th century was a time of great change in interior decoration, with the appearance of a new love of harmony and symmetry in design, and a new concept of furnishings designed to relate to each other in a pleasing composition. Mme de Rambouillet amazed the sophisticated world when she redecorated her Parisian apartments in a design that involved not only painting all the walls blue, but also having all the furnishings, including wall hangings, window curtains and table carpets, woven in tones of blue and gold to match.

France and Italy vied with each other as innovators, and slowly their ideas of harmony and symmetry were exported to other countries, including Holland and England. Craftsmen, too, were more mobile than before, and those who went to northern countries found an appreciative audience.

Fashionable English interiors were soon modeled on the French ideal. For example, leaded lights, so popular throughout Tudor times, went out of fashion in the 1630s, and windows with wooden struts then began to take their place. Internal shutters were still used both in England and in Holland – now often set in pairs, and sometimes in vertical tiers. Curtains were not to be widespread until the 18th century, but they were already becoming more popular. A few grand houses had paired draw curtains with deep, padded cornices in the French and Italian manner. However, curtains were usually single. They were made of fairly transparent silk, taffeta or linen, attached by means of rings to a narrow pole.

As the 17th century progressed, the design of the bed became more sophisticated. Still usually shaped like a box, its posts now often had wooden finials carved with decorative themes, ranging from plumes of feathers to winged birds. In Continental Europe, beds sometimes had canopies of corniced and fringed hangings that rose into rounded domes or sharp points.

The generous hangings of this period were made in wonderful cloth. Italy's textile industry was constantly creating new fabrics: especially favored were luxury silks and velvets with large floral patterns. At the same time the workshops of France produced velvets extravagantly interwoven with precious metals and silks.

THE LATER 17TH CENTURY

In the middle of the 17th century, the French court became hugely influential. When the palace of Versailles was being created, between 1660 and 1680, descriptions of its marvels influenced wealthy house owners, not only in France, but in England and Holland too. At Versailles everything was designed to reflect the Sun King's

magnificence, dignity and power. Even the colors used were regal–rich purples, golds and blacks. From Charles I down the social ladder, the English sought to emulate the taste and skills of the French, but the results lacked Gallic finesse. English interiors were colorful and bright, but cruder than the original inspiration, until England benefited from the influx of refugee craftsmen from France in the 1680s. Nevertheless, the English houses were very comfortably furnished. The walls and doors were hung with matching fabrics, and the same fabrics were hung on the beds. The need for mobile tapestries had disappeared: after the Restoration, walls were for the first time covered with fixed hangings – not only tapestries, but woven damasks, watered silks and other lighter

△

IN EUROPE IN THE 17TH AND 18TH CENTURIES, A MAGNIFICENT RANGE OF RICH, HIGHLY TEXTURED FABRICS WAS AVAILABLE FOR WINDOW DRESSINGS IN THE HOMES OF THE WEALTHY. BRAIDS AND BORDERS WERE COMPLEX AND LUXURIOUS, AND EVEN THE SIMPLEST OF SHAPES WERE TRIMMED IN A REGAL MANNER. THE DETAILS ABOVE EVOKE SOMETHING OF THE SPLENDOR OF THIS GOLDEN AGE OF FABRICS. INTERESTING EXAMPLES SURVIVE IN GRAND HOMES TODAY. HOWEVER, MANY HISTORIC FABRICS HAVE SUFFERED FROM THE RAVAGES OF TIME AND HAVE HAD TO BE REPLACED BY COPIES IN INFERIOR MATERIALS. ONE OF THE MAJOR CENTERS WAS GENOA, WHICH PRODUCED HIGH-QUALITY HEAVY SILKS AND VELVETS FOR FURNISHINGS UNTIL THE LATE 18TH CENTURY. VENICE WAS KNOWN FOR ITS FINE BROCADES.

◁ ▽

TODAY'S FASHION FOR BED HANGINGS DERIVES FROM A TRADITION THAT RUNS RIGHT FROM THE MIDDLE AGES THROUGH TO THE 19TH CENTURY. IN THE 17TH CENTURY, THE BED BECAME LESS OF A DRAFT-PROOF BOX AND MORE OF A STATUS SYMBOL, WITH SILK DAMASKS AND BROCADES LOOPED AND FESTOONED INTO INCREDIBLE SHAPES. ENGLISH BEDS (LIKE THAT IN THE MIDDLE EXAMPLE HERE) WERE SIMPLER IN THEIR HANGINGS THAN THEIR CONTINENTAL COUNTERPARTS. HALF- OR FULL-CANOPIES SHOWED THE TURNED WOOD OF THE POSTS TO BEST ADVANTAGE. THE THIRD EXAMPLE (BELOW) IS A FRENCH DOME BED OF 1826: THIS STYLE OF IMPERIAL SOLEMNITY, NAPOLEONIC IN ORIGIN, MADE ITS IMPACT ON BOTH ENGLAND AND AMERICA.

fabrics. These were the forerunners of the wallpapers of the next century.

In France, Louis XIV had established the silk industry in Lyons, whose looms produced smooth silks, taffetas, ribbed silks, *moirés,* brocades, damasks and satins, and elaborate fringing. These were used on upholstery, hangings and state beds across Europe.

The bed was still the main focus of decorative ingenuity. The grandest English and French houses had a state or ceremonial bed – a symbol of a family's standing and position in the community. Because of what it represented, it was expensively and elaborately ornamented. The cost could be enormous.

The bed began to lose its closed box look. The upper frame was carved, and the curtains descending from beneath it were lighter, sometimes raised in festoons instead of drawn. Grand beds would sometimes be half-canopies with silk curtains and valances, perhaps draped and looped into more festoons. Cornices and valances were embroidered and bordered with gold and silver thread or with woven silks, and hangings were appliquéed with motifs in green, violet, pink, or white.

A new design became fashionable: the *à la duchesse* or angel bed. This had a flying canopy that was hung from the ceiling rather than being supported by posts. Further departures from the box bed came about under the influence of Daniel Marot, a French designer who settled in Holland. In 1684 he published engravings showing designs for state beds which, despite their severely classical lines, were infinitely more complex than anything that had gone before, and which had a great influence on bed hangings for the next twenty years.

At last the humble window curtain became an essential part of the decorative scheme. Simple styles disappeared, influenced by the grandeur of the French beds with their heavy cornices and valances and the festooned wall hangings which often complemented them. Across Europe, paired curtains were now established, first hung on their own, and then headed with simple cornices designed to hide the fittings.
Fabric at the window no longer served merely to control light. Window dressing came into being, with ruched valances softening the tops of windows. In the 1680s pull-up curtains began to appear. Their cord-and-pulley mechanism created an effect similar to that of an Austrian shade, and the top was hidden behind a cornice.

A LIGHT ROCOCO MOOD, EXEMPLIFIED IN THIS
LOUIS XV DINING ROOM, SPREAD FROM FRANCE
ACROSS EUROPE. CURTAINS TENDED TO BECOME
LESS FORMAL, AND SOMETIMES ALMOST PLAYFUL
IN CHARACTER.

▷

THIS PAGE, RIGHT THESE MID-19TH CENTURY
BALDAQUINS (CANOPIES) ARE AN EXAGGERATED
RECREATION OF LOUIS XV EXUBERANCE.

▽

THE CHOICE OF FABRICS WAS IMMENSE IN THE
18TH CENTURY—WITH SILKS FROM LYONS AND
BROCADES FROM ITALY. THE GRANDEUR OF THE
PERIOD IS TELLINGLY CONVEYED IN THIS ROOM OF
MELLOW RED AND GOLD, WHERE WALL COVERINGS
AND CURTAINS BLEND TOGETHER.

THE 18TH CENTURY

Inevitably in France there was a reaction against the ceremonious Baroque style of the Sun King, Louis XIV. A new reign and a new century heralded a new mood – a sense of increased informality and gaiety, which expressed itself in the Rococo style.

Variety, elegance and a harmonious lightness, epitomized by the paintings of Watteau, were the keynotes of this delightful fantasy. The light Rococo mood touched everything – textiles, curtains, beds and other furniture – with its airy garlands of flowers, knots of ribbons, and other natural forms such as foliage and flowers – often with a touch of Chinese influence *(chinoiserie)*.

England and America were less affected by the frivolity of the Rococo, although there was a flirtation with fantasy Gothick in the middle of the century. More influential was the elegant Neo-classical Palladian style, promulgated by the architect and designer William Kent whose grand tour had brought him into contact with the classical villas of Andrea Palladio outside Venice.

Meanwhile, fabrics became yet more plentiful. Cloths included printed cotton chintzes from India, for use in country houses. In 1752 Francis Nixon, in Ireland, used an engraved copper plate to print cotton with fast colors, and other European makers soon followed suit. In France the factories of Lyons turned out ever more charming designs in woven silk – light silks with scattered posies and in new, pale colors such as pink and sky-blue. Italy was still producing furnishing silks – rich damasks, velvets and brocades, many with large floral patterns. From the Far East, painted silks were imported to be used as fixed wall hangings in town houses, nailed to a frame and masked by a border.

Fabrics also became more sophisticated in composition. Silk was mixed with linen or cotton for a range of damasks, and there were *moirés* and velvets, and all sorts of worsted materials. However, the use of fabrics for wall hangings diminished: instead, wallpapers in imitation of fabric were beginning to be seen, and a feeling was growing for the lighter look of painted paneling.

English and American beds were still fairly box-like in shape, while French beds were more ornate – for example, there was the fashionable *polonaise* bed, set lengthwise across the wall and surmounted by a small dome. It was France too

that saw the introduction of a bed in a recess – known as a Turkish bed – which provided new opportunities for the use of fabric.

Bed hangings had reached their apotheosis. Elaborate canopies and cornices curved in waves. The curtains, whether drawn on poles or looped and festooned into a pull-up style, were of lighter fabrics. Special embroideries for bed curtains were being designed by Huquier and Pillement in France, using bright silks, and gold and silver threads.

Eventually, after the 1740s, beds and their hangings became less innovative as their design passed into the hands of the cabinetmaker, and out of the influence of the upholsterer.

By the 18th century, most windows had curtains. Despite the new pull-up curtains, divided curtains were still current. Both types used ample fabric and had cornices, often embellished with bands and insets of embroidery. The festoon, moreover, had arrived: originally conceived as a transparent sun curtain that could be raised above the window, sitting beneath a cornice, it now came in a variety of light shimmering silks. Indeed, few curtains were made of heavy material.

Light-excluding sash curtains were still in use –essentially shades set on a frame that fitted inside the window. Other kinds of shades grew in popularity throughout the 18th century. Mme de Pompadour had a painted Italian taffeta roller blind in 1755. Shades were common in Italy, and by the 1770s venetian blinds were used in England.

The tailed curtain also came into being at this time. Paired curtains were fitted with pulls so that they drew diagonally up and apart, so that the outer edge hung in a point down the side of the window. Also known as reefed curtains, these were the forerunners of the tails often used on curtains today.

The 1760s saw a new wave of Neo-classicism, nurtured by the excavators' findings at the ancient sites of Pompeii and Herculaneum. This disciplined classicism, inspired by antiquity itself rather than by the long classical tradition, was more austere than before. In England Robert Adam emerged as the influential figure, and was appointed architect to George III. Formal motifs, urns, tripods and masks appeared on everything. The lines were clean, cool and harmonious.

In the Neo-classical interiors, curtains were

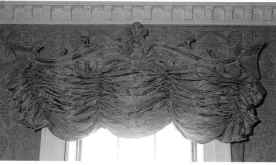

made in soft, light-colored fabrics–silk, damasks and brocatelles in quiet floral designs; taffetas with watered or brocaded stripes; velvet, voile and muslin. The palette ranged from crimson to green and daffodil yellow, and new colors were introduced–royal blue, turquoise and violet.

Curtains, though of disciplined design, were increasingly opulent, topped by symmetrically draped festoons as well as cornices, and secured on the walls by cloak pins. The festoons usually consisted of one or two swags, with carefully proportioned tails at either side, often trimmed with a Neo-classical motif. The cornices were surmounted by classical plaster decoration, often very intricate.

Draw curtains were now in much grander form. In England and America they were called French rod curtains. Instead of merely joining, they overlapped at the center, operated by a system of cords and pulleys. Thomas Chippendale – who interested himself in curtains as much as in other aspects of furniture – designed heavy carved wooden cornices for these new types of curtains. A much grander look had emerged.

◁ ◁

THIS PRINT OF 1787 (THIS PAGE, FAR LEFT) SHOWS THREE DESIGNS FOR NEO-CLASSICAL MOLDINGS TO BE USED OVER EITHER BEDS OR WINDOWS. MOTIFS OF THIS PERIOD DERIVED FROM A RENEWED INTEREST IN ANTIQUITY. THE URN WAS A FAVORITE SYMBOL, UBIQUITOUS IN THE INTERIORS OF THE TIME: NOTE THE UPRIGHT AND FLATTENED FORMS OF URN IN THE FIRST AND SECOND OF THESE DESIGNS. THE THIRD EXAMPLE FEATURES ANOTHER POPULAR SYMBOL, THE RAM'S HEAD. BOTH THESE MOTIFS DERIVE FROM ANCIENT ROME.

◁

THERE WAS A TENDENCY IN THE 18TH AND EARLY 19TH CENTURIES TO USE ELABORATE DECORATION AT THE TOP OF A WINDOW ARRANGEMENT–FOR EXAMPLE, AN ORNATE CORNICE HANGING FROM A MOLDING CARVED WITH CLASSICAL MOTIFS. SOME EXAMPLES FROM THE REPERTOIRE OF TYPICAL ORNAMENT ARE SHOWN IN THE PHOTOGRAPHS ON THIS PAGE, RANGING FROM A SWAGGED, HEAVILY GILDED MOLDING (TOP), THROUGH TWO DEEPLY FESTOONED VALANCES, TO AN IMPOSING SCALLOP SHELL ABOVE A PORTIÈRE (BOTTOM).

EMPIRE AND REGENCY STYLES

What came to be known as the Empire style came into being in Paris at the end of the 18th century, after the French Revolution. It was profoundly influenced by Napoleon and his Imperial career – particularly his Egyptian campaign – and by the excavations of antiquities at Pompeii and Herculaneum. The style outlasted its Napoleonic origins and, with modifications, spread through mainland Europe. Essentially, it was a continuation of Neo-classicism, but now pieces of furniture and decoration were painstakingly copied from the newly discovered paintings and sculptures of Ancient Rome and Egypt.

The English version of the Empire style was the Regency style. This too was based on classical designs, but its character was plainer and simpler, with less relief ornament, and with the emphasis on Ancient Greek motifs. Thomas Hope was its mastermind.

The early 19th century gave more importance to curtains and draperies than they had ever had before. The ideas introduced at this period remained influential for the rest of the century and still affect our curtain designs today.

French upholsterers were very inventive, and their designs were shown all over Europe. In England, one of the most influential people was publisher Rudolph Ackermann, who in 1809 began to produce a magazine called *The Repository of Arts*. This not only showed styles for curtains and drapes, but also introduced a startling innovation – the use of real fabric samples, stuck onto the pages of each issue.

The basic curtains in the rather severe Empire style were floor-length draw curtains. The festoon curtain, too bulky now for any but the largest windows and rooms, was considered very *démodé*. However, simple draw curtains were very adaptable, and they could be bunched into ties and set off with drapery – an increasingly fashionable element of a window.

A simple drapery consisted of one, two or three swags with single tails at either end. The intersections were sometimes defined with heavy tassels, and the curves of the swags outlined with fringing. As the style progressed, the swags became more voluminous, sometimes taking the form of lengths of fabric flung across a pole. Continuous drapery was introduced to link two or more windows on a single wall.

△
DEEP SWAGS ARE ONE OF THE IDEAS BORROWED FROM THE EMPIRE STYLE IN PERIOD ROOMS TODAY—ESPECIALLY THOSE WITH TALL WINDOWS.

△
THIS POLE AND DRAPERY DESIGN OF 1806, PUBLISHED IN LONDON, SHOWS THE CONTINUING INFLUENCE OF *CHINOISERIE* IN ITS DRAGON MOTIFS. POLES WERE PROUDLY DISPLAYED AT THIS PERIOD, AND BECAME HIGHLY ORNATE.

△
TOP LEFT THE REGENCY STYLE STARTED IN A RELATIVELY SEVERE MANNER, BUT SOON ACQUIRED VARIOUS EMBELLISHMENTS—PARTICULARLY IN THE WINDOW DRESSINGS, POISED BETWEEN GEORGIAN PURITY AND THE FURBELOWS OF THE LATER 19TH CENTURY.

▷
OPPOSITE PAGE THESE TWO ROOMS IN AN ENGLISH HOUSE CONTAIN FORMAL, RESTRAINED CURTAIN TREATMENTS IN DEEP TONES. IN VICTORIA'S REIGN, THE ELEGANCE OF THIS LATE CLASSICAL STYLE WAS TO GIVE WAY TO LESS DISCIPLINED FASHIONS.

The poles were now on view, so these had to be decorated too. Poles were usually molded and gilded, the finials and brackets finished with animals' heads, anthemiona (floral designs) and other classically inspired motifs. Gilt rosettes, laurel wreaths or proud eagles sometimes caught the fabric lightly in the center.

Plaster moldings were introduced as an alternative to decorative poles. These were elaborate decorations, painted or gilded, and often had stiffened, shaped fabric valances or cornices beneath. The cornices themselves were sometimes plain, sometimes festooned, but never simple. They were usually trimmed with bows and rosettes.

At first, the curtains beneath these fine headings were simple enough, though artfully pinned or tied back at the sides to form elegant swags. However, very soon they became more complex, while always remaining formal. For the first time, undercurtains of a light muslin or silk were used with heavier outer curtains. Sometimes the outer curtains were dress curtains, for display only, and not designed to draw. As time progressed, the inner curtains were often also coupled with lightweight shades. Shades with painted decoration were fairly common, and spring-operated shades were now frequently seen.

Many plain curtains had wide, rich fabric borders or embroidery borders. Bees, crowns, stars, roses and rosettes were all popular motifs. There was a splendid variety of trimmings at this time: to reduce expense, professionally made trimmings were imitated by ladies at home, many of whom fringed and knotted their own beds and curtains. In time, fringes were to become deeper and heavier, and tassels more elaborate. However, the basic styles of fringes and tassels created in this era remain with us today, remarkably unaltered.

Beds were still dressed to fit in with the overall decoration of the room, but they became simpler and lighter. In France the couch bed, with its classically curved ends, was *de rigueur,* and lent itself to austerely elegant settings. Often placed against a wall at this period, the bed had a canopy, with curtains below, the symmetrical swags punctuated with the same grand Imperial devices as those on the window dressing. Many designs were published, to be imitated in great numbers in America.

The range of fabric types and colors now available was as great as history would ever see— Genoa silks, silks from Lyons and elsewhere, velvets in wool, cotton and silk, damasks in silk, wool-and-silk and linen, lustrous taffetas, and ribbed silks with a glitter finish. Some fabrics were patterned with scenes of human figures and animals, and printed linens were very fashionable. Colors were strong, and were sometimes bright. For the sprigged muslin inner curtains, saffron, deep pink, cherry and green were among the popular alternatives.

THE 19TH CENTURY

The year that Queen Victoria married Prince Albert – 1840 – usefully marks the time of a huge change in style between the early and later 19th century. This is as true of America as it is of England. America in the 19th century had a new and expanding middle class who used their houses to advertise their recently acquired status. Under pressure from this shift in social structure, the stylistic simplicity of the early 1800s gave way to increasing elaboration.

Novelty, in abundance, was the quality that was craved. A confusion of styles and revivals began to emerge, obscuring what had gone before. Tables were covered with heavy cloths and bric-à-brac; furniture gained loose covers, buttoned backs, cushions and antimacassars; pianos, notoriously, were draped to spare the blushes of the prudish; and curtains, in chemically dyed fabrics and with lavish braids and trimmings, disproportionately deep swags and over-ornamented, over-large poles, were now the most prominent components in interiors that were decorated to excess. Rooms became darker because of the weight and quantity of fabric used at windows, and in some cases light was kept out altogether by the addition of shades kept half-drawn.

The 19th-century lady had new sources of advice. She was helped not only by the ever-resourceful upholsterer, but also by the many books now published on the new mechanized presses, suggesting elaborate designs for hanging and draping windows.

The restrained swagged and draped styles of the early part of the century were now greatly embellished. Arrangements were fringed, braided and bobbled, and were fixed rather than adjustable. Outer curtains were permanently drawn across at the top and hooked back at the sides to form huge, heavy loops of fabric. Beneath were lighter curtains of muslin or lace, and often, behind these, small curtains of muslin or net, fitted against the window, known as glass

THE 19TH CENTURY VALUED LIGHT AND AIR MUCH LESS THAN WE DO TODAY. DEEP, SOMBER CURTAINS IN TOWNHOUSES OF THIS PERIOD OFTEN CREATED A SHADOWY HALF-LIGHT.

curtains. Fashionable windows were additionally fitted with roller shades. Painted or printed with designs or made of woven, self-patterned fabrics, shades were trimmed with fringes or perhaps openwork borders.

Brass poles were manufactured in many different lengths and widths – some as thick as an arm – and were fashionable for swags and drapes. Cornices lost the simplicity of earlier designs, and were edged with thick fringing, often with a separate central swathe of fabric over them. A strange extension of the cornice that developed during this period was the lambrequin, essentially a flat cornice of curved or shaped outline which continued down the sides of the window – sometimes reaching as far as the floor. Initially used in Italy, as a way to hide the bunches of fabric that formed when a pull-up curtain was drawn above the window, the lambrequin had at first functioned as a window dressing in itself, with just a simple muslin

curtain beneath. Now, however, it was combined with symmetrical main curtains below and, often, an asymmetrical muslin one as well – all caught in different tie-backs.

Silk wall hangings continued to be used in formal rooms, but heavily patterned wallpapers had taken over in the bedroom. In the 1840s and 50s, beds were dressed in much the same way as windows. In fashionable bedrooms the window curtains were supposed to match the hangings surrounding the bed. Later, as iron and brass beds were substituted for wooden ones, the half-canopy generally replaced the full-canopy above the bed, and it was felt to be more healthy to sleep without layers of draperies all around.

Hangings in other parts of a room became heavier and more abundant. Doors, and even archways, were hung with heavy portières. Contrived draperies decorated looking glasses, and sometimes even the mantelpiece as well. Nowhere (except the bed) was safe from the seas of fabric.

The preferred colors were intense and deep. Red was the most favored color of all–so long as it was dark and rich. Fabrics were weighty, with damask, moreen, repp (a fabric with a corded surface) and brocades much in vogue.

By the 1890s, all proportion and symmetry had been lost. Pompous and pretentious, bulky and heavy, these curtain treatments strutted their way to the century's end, until the inevitable swing of the pendulum back toward purism and simplicity.

THE 20TH CENTURY

In the later 19th century, a minority reaction against excess in interior design became firmly entrenched. In England, William Morris and Charles Eastlake had been sounding the battle cry since the 1860s. The architect A.W.N. Pugin and the designer Owen Jones (author of the influential *Grammar of Ornament*) belonged to the same movement of thought. Simpler styling took some time to arrive, but by the 1890s there was a perceptible shift in taste. This was linked with certain decorative fashions, most notably the vogue for Japanese design, which reigned from the 1870s on, gaining momentum from the opening of Arthur Lazenby Liberty's stores in London in 1875 and Paris in 1889. Also influential were the romanticized Gothic and quaint Old English styles. Each of these fashions

TOWARD THE END OF THE 19TH CENTURY, SINUOUS PLANT FORMS BEGAN TO APPEAR IN FABRICS AND FURNISHINGS, MARKING THE EMERGENCE OF ART NOUVEAU.

GOTHIC WAS A MAJOR INSPIRATION IN THE 19TH CENTURY. THE REVIVAL OF THE CHIVALRIC IDEAL LED TO MOCK-MEDIEVAL WINDOW DRESSINGS SUCH AS THIS ONE, WITH LAMBREQUINS.

THE RENAISSANCE, A PERIOD OF RAPID PROGRESS IN CIVILIZATION, WAS ANOTHER SOURCE OF INSPIRATION TO DESIGNERS OF CURTAIN ARRANGEMENTS IN THE 19TH CENTURY.

played a part in simplifying the role of the curtain. Gradually, the idea of an ornate fabric construction at the window lost its appeal, and began to be viewed as old-fashioned.

Much has been written about William Morris and his medievalist disciples, and the value they gave to the pure and simple. Morris was, and still is, vastly influential in the field of interior decoration. His insistence on using natural forms, translated into flat patterns, started a whole new way of looking at fabric. These patterns replaced the overblown, "naturalistic" designs of the time, and heavy fabrics gave way to printed linens and cottons.

A parallel approach was extended to furniture and to architecture under the umbrella of the Arts and Crafts movement, which made simplicity of design fashionable in some quarters in the 1890s. Popular taste generally did not go quite as far as the Morris disciples would have wished, but at least the emphasis had shifted. As

far as curtains were concerned, the shift was partly in response to the smaller windows of new houses. Perhaps also, people simply wanted to see out of their windows again.

A factor that was to become more and more important for curtaining as the 20th century took hold was that fewer girls were willing to go into domestic service. The factories offered an alluring alternative. Even more attractive were the options created by the growth of commercial business and the giant new department stores. The difficulty of obtaining skilled home labor for sewing helped to encourage simplicity in window treatments. At the same time, influenced by modern ideas about health, and the new washing machines which helped people put these ideas into practice, washable fabrics displaced the heavy velvets and brocades.

The 20th century heralded a new excitement in pattern and color, whose impetus is still with us today. It also brought an accelerating pace of

and the use of artificial fibers (the first viscose technological change – not only mass-production yarn was exhibited at the Paris International Exhibition in 1900) but also developments in dyes and dyeing techniques, and in the printing of textiles. Art movements such as Constructivism, Cubism and, in the 1960s, Pop Art had their successive influences on pattern.

Curtain treatments for windows reached a nadir of dullness after the Second World War. On the standard arrangement of a simple pair of curtains, with sheers (or "nets") behind for privacy, there were few interesting variations. The problem of curtaining, for example, a picture window successfully was a challenge to which few could rise.

Today, the situation is much healthier. The styles of the past have cross-fertilized with a spirit of post-modern adventure to produce a wealth of window and bed treatments in homes of every style.

△

THE EGYPTIAN STYLE OF NAPOLEONIC FRANCE
CAN WORK WELL IN A PERIOD HOUSE. IN THIS
ASYMMETRICAL DRESSING, THE KEYNOTE IS SET BY
A BOLD COLOR SCHEME AND BY PAPYRUS MOTIFS
ON THE CORNICE AND THE OUTER DRAPES. THE
CORNICE IS CUT TO SHOW A SOFT VALANCE WITH
HEAVY TASSELS.

▷

THE STYLE HERE IS ONE OF RICH, FORMAL
SIMPLICITY. FRINGED RED SILK HAS BEEN DRAPED
OVER A BLACK POLE TO FORM SWAGS AND TAILS.
THE LIGHTER INNER CURTAINS ARE TIED BACK AT
THE LOWEST POINT OF THE RED TAILS: THIS HELPS
TO UNIFY THE DESIGN. BEHIND IS A SHEER
AUSTRIAN SHADE.

It is difficult to find anything new among today's most fashionable curtain arrangements. Even if your wish is for the simplest of cottons or linens, just hung on a plain brass rail or rod, you are only emulating the first curtains, back in the days when function was all-important and style irrelevant.

Inevitably, the past offers a rich source of inspiration for the curtains of today. Historic paintings and prints provide endless ideas for treating windows and beds. To a great extent, these elements borrowed from history are filtered through the medium of personal taste. The same look – say, French Empire – will be interpreted completely differently by any two individuals. The fabrics used, the colors chosen, and the overall shape of the composition, will reflect the owner's personality in subtle, indefinable ways. Taste is infinitely various, because it is not ready-made: it develops in us from an early age, influenced by a complex tangle of our experiences and memories.

Apart from such imponderables, which make every room unique, there are certain more tangible factors that will help to determine the treatment of fabrics in a room. Various questions have to be asked. What is the function of the room? How important is the degree of natural light admitted? Is there a strong architectural style which the curtains, shades or drapes must complement?

A golden rule is to treat the curtainings as an integral part of the overall decoration of the room. Often, they are the focal point of the interior, the element that has strongest visual impact. In style, they should harmonize with the walls, floor treatment, furnishings and furniture. If you ignore this principle, you run the risk of creating an effect that is vaguely unsettling: if you take it fully into account, you are well on the way to creating a home that is welcoming and attractive in every room.

▷

A SIMPLE STYLE OF CURTAINING IN YELLOW COTTON WITH A PATTERNED GRAY BORDER ALONG THE INSIDE EDGES (TO ECHO THE CEILING CORNICE), AND ROPE TIE-BACKS, WAS THE CHOICE FOR THE ANGLED BAY OF THIS BEDROOM. THE AUSTERITY OF THIS APPROACH CONTRASTS WITH THE LACQUERED FURNITURE AND FLORAL RUG. SUCH ECLECTIC MIXES CAN WORK WELL IF YOU PERFORM THEM WITH PANACHE.

△

OPULENCE IS CREATED HERE BY A RICH MIXTURE OF PATTERNS AND COLORS. THE PINCH-PLEATED CURTAINS (BOTH PAIRS HUNG FROM A SINGLE ROD) ARE IN BURGUNDY TONES THAT HARMONIZE WELL WITH THE WALLPAPER, WHOSE BUSY SMALL-SCALE PATTERN CONTRASTS WITH THE LARGE-SCALE PAISLEY PATTERN OF THE FABRIC. A FURTHER CONTRAST IS CREATED BY THE FIGURED LACE ROLLER SHADES. ON EACH WINDOW THE OUTER CURTAINS ARE MATCHED WITH AN INNER SWAG OF FABRIC JUST VISIBLE AT THE V-SHAPED JOINTS.

Formal curtains can be used today to create an impression of luxury in more modest rooms – even those decorated in keeping with today's subtle tastes. They are usually floor-length and full, often held back with a fabric tie or cord or metal clip. They may be surmounted by a valance, or by swags and drapes, and sometimes decorated with braids, ropes and cords. Bows can be used to good effect.

Although formal curtains look their best in rooms with high ceilings and tall windows, they can look convincing in any room so long as the proportions are right and there is enough area of wall and ceiling to balance the display of fabric. Do not be tempted to use them in a room that is too narrow or too small, or has low ceilings or awkward corners. Irregularly shaped rooms need something less ordered.

Formal curtains must also go well with the furniture. That does not mean that if you are using grand curtains in a historic style, the furniture has to be in period – only that, whether old or new, the furniture must match the curtains in visual weight.

The showcase rooms of the house – such as the living room and dining room – are obvious locations, but you can often afford to be more adventurous. Usually, the kitchen is not an option: the contrast of formal statement and practical function would be unsettling.

It is important to choose the right weight and style of fabric. The so-called traditional fabrics usually look best – damasks, velvets, heavy silks and cottons, and plain and printed linens.

The choice of fabric design is influenced by the cut and hang of the particular style of arrangement. Stripes of all widths work well, as do checks and flowery chintzes, linens and silks. Plain fabrics and those with a self-pattern can be effective, or perhaps a combination of fabrics – possibly including a contrasting edge or lining. Interestingly, many designs and colors that we enjoy now were scorned a century ago. Elsie de Wolfe, the American interior decorator, writing in 1910, congratulates herself on the success of her dedicated battle to reintroduce patterned chintzes, which were very unfashionable, to her ultra-fashionable clientele.

Formality is about classical perfection and attention to detail: this is not the occasion on which to experiment with makeshift arrangements.

△

THE EARLY 19TH-CENTURY UPHOLSTERER
GEORGE SMITH WAS FAMOUS FOR HIS
COMPLICATED CURTAIN DESIGNS. THIS ONE FOR A
DRAWING ROOM COMBINES MANY FASHIONABLE
ELEMENTS OF THE DAY. THE HUGE BRASS POLE
WITH ELABORATE FINIALS IS CAPPED BY A
MILITARISTIC CENTRAL DEVICE. THE ORNATE
SWAGS IN BLUE BACKED WITH RED HAVE FRINGES,
AND FLOOR-LENGTH TAILS AT EITHER SIDE.

△△

TOP SUMPTUOUS SILK CURTAINS WITH A NARROW
PENCIL-PLEAT HEADING ARE CROSSED AT THE TOP
BY DEEP FESTOONING SWAGS, RICHLY FRINGED.
SIMPLE CROSS-SHAPED ROSETTES BREAK THE TOP
LINE OF THE COMPOSITION.

◁

THE SWAGS AND TAILS OF THIS BAY WINDOW
COMPOSITION HANG DIRECTLY FROM THE CEILING
MOLDING. THE SYMMETRICAL DOUBLE TAILS IN THE
CENTER (ONE INSIDE THE OTHER) ARE TOPPED
WITH ROSETTES, WHILE THE LONGER AND
BROADER OUTER TAILS HAVE ROSETTES ON THE
CORNERS. THE CURTAINS THEMSELVES ARE EACH
CAUGHT BY A SIMPLE ROPE SECURED BEHIND THE
TAILS. THE MUSHROOM LINING AND DARKER
BROWN TRIM WORK WELL WITH THE CREAM.

△

ANOTHER FORMAL BAY WINDOW TREATMENT THAT
DEPENDS ON SUBTLE COLORING AND MAKES
OPTIMUM USE OF A CEILING MOLDING. NARROW
HEAVY COTTON CURTAINS IN A STRIPED PATTERN
FRAME EACH DIVISION OF THE WINDOW, WITHOUT
TIE-BACKS. THE HEADING IS RELATIVELY SIMPLE,
WITH FULL SWAGS AND BROAD TAILS LINED WITH A
PLAIN CONTRAST FABRIC. THE CENTRAL CURTAINS
ARE NARROW ENOUGH TO PREVENT THE LOSS OF
TOO MUCH DAYLIGHT.

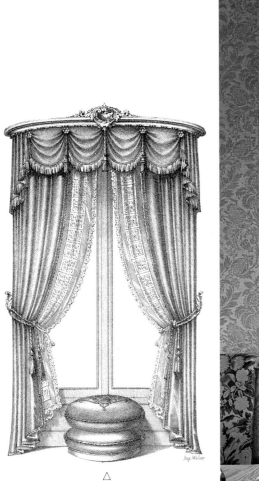

△

A Louis XV dressing. From the
ceiling molding, curved away
from the wall, hangs an
elaborate valance, swagged,
fringed and caught with little
rosettes. The outer curtains in
the same fabric are echoed in
shape by undercurtains.

A STUNNING PARTNERSHIP OF BALLOON SHADES WITH SWAGS AND TAILS IN THE SAME STRIPED SILK FABRIC. THE SWAGS ARE FORMED ON THREE BRASS ROSETTES WHICH ECHO THE GILDING ON THE PILASTERS AND CORNICE. SWAGS, TAILS AND SHADE ARE ALL EDGED WITH A TWO-COLOR FRINGE, AND THE RED LINING GIVES EXTRA IMPACT TO THE TAILS.

ABOVE LEFT SIMPLE FRENCH-PLEATED COTTON CURTAINS ARE HEADED WITH A PATTERN OF ROPES AND TASSELS THREADED THROUGH THE CURTAIN RINGS: THIS GIVES A FORMAL AIR, WITHOUT EXCESSIVE WEIGHT. THE CURTAINS ARE CAUGHT BACK AT A HIGHER POINT THAN USUAL, AND ARE PERMANENTLY FASTENED IN THE CENTER AT A BOW TO WHICH ALL THE ROPES CONVERGE.

THIS FAIRLY STRAIGHTFORWARD TREATMENT OF SWAGS AND TAILS IS ENRICHED BY THE USE OF A RICH DAMASK THAT GOES WELL WITH THE BEAUTIFUL PATTERN OF THE SOFA. THE TAILS ARE FRINGED AND LINED SO THAT THEY STAND OUT AGAINST THE FULLNESS OF FABRIC BEHIND, WHILE THE SWAGS HANG AGAINST A NARROWLY PLEATED VALANCE IN A NEUTRAL COLOR.

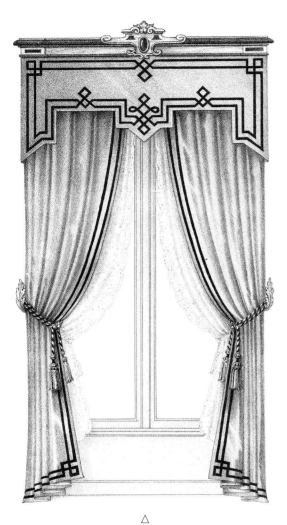

△

A SEVERE TREATMENT IN WHICH THE UNUSUAL SHAPE OF THE CORNICE IS HIGHLIGHTED BY AN ELABORATELY CRISS-CROSSING BORDER OF NARROW BANDS, ECHOED ON THE CURTAINS THEMSELVES.

Drama is an essential part of interior decoration. A house or room totally devoid of drama will remain flat, lacking in interest. There is a need, of course, for quiet and relaxing elements in any house, but other areas demand a treatment that is eyecatching and assertive. To work well as a whole, an interior needs pace and variety. The obvious approach would be to treat the hall and main living area with a degree of flamboyance and to make other parts of the house more reticent in mood. However, the obvious strategies are not necessarily the best ones. Even a bedroom, traditionally the room where softness and tranquility are the keynotes, may benefit from a bolder touch.

In the classic style of theater, the moment of peak excitement is when the curtains first majestically part to reveal the world onstage. Grand opera houses often capitalize on the sense of anticipation with simple deep red velvet drapes, fringed with gold – massive folds of fabric, which, when they sweep apart, bunch into confident curves. Transferring the theatrical style to curtains in the home requires care: the intention is to make a flourish, not overwhelm. In rooms that are in constant use, bold statements may become tiresomely dominant. On the other hand, in a little-used room there is a risk that the impact might be wasted.

Proportion, as always, is a key factor. Ensure that the area of valance and drapes is precisely judged in relation to the walls. Dramatic curtains look best in certain types of rooms and with certain types of windows. They associate particularly well with tall, classically proportioned windows, which often demand swags and tails. The room should be large enough to accommodate the curtains without a sense of visual discomfort. A small, nondescript room will look even smaller if the curtains are given emphatic treatment. There should always be enough light to show the curtains off to good advantage. A room in which there are many small windows is clearly not the right place for high drama. Neither, perhaps surprisingly, is a room with too many large windows: in this situation it is important not to overdo things.

Dramatic curtains must always be full. Never be tempted to skimp on fabric. Fullness will allow your curtains to flow, loop and curve. They should stride, not tiptoe. Don't forget the trick of using an unexpected gesture to catch the attention – for example, a heavy rope holding the curtain back, double-sized tassels on a tie-back, curtains permanently joined at the center, or a brightly colored lining brought unexpectedly around the front. If you trust your own taste unwaveringly, you could even get away with a contrast of patterns – perhaps, one in the curtains, one in Roman shades behind.

A happy choice of fabric and color is imperative. For maximum richness of effect try a fabric shot with two colors, or a deep-piled fabric such as velvet, chenille, or even felt. Avoid small prints, which will create little more than a blurred impression when spread over a large area. You might consider highly colorful chintz – perhaps a scattering of exotic birds or trailing vines and flowers. Stripes are a good choice, whether bold and deep against a neutral background or color-toned in shades across the spectrum. A plain rich or unusual color in an unexpected fabric can look marvelous.

Crimson, emerald, yellow and blue are all effective. Tie-backs, borders and valances picked out in opposite tones always draw the eye.

Drama implies dash, not haste. To bring off a dramatic window dressing, you need to put plenty of effort into both planning and execution, and to pay attention to the details. In a composition designed to be eye-catching, any mistake in the proportion, the color, the fabric choice or the shape will be all too noticeable. However, in the conception as a whole, it is crucial that you should not be too reticent. The most important ingredients of all are imagination and confidence – and perhaps a sprinkling of wit.

▷

A DRAMATIC ARRANGEMENT THAT USES GEOMETRY IN A MODERN CONTEXT. AGAIN, BORDERS ARE USED TO DEFINE AN INTERESTING SHAPE. THE CURTAINS ARE IN HEAVY WHITE COTTON, TRIMMED IN A DARK BLUE THAT ALMOST LOOKS BLACK IN CERTAIN LIGHTS. PLAIN SHEERS BEHIND PROVIDE A UNIFORM BACKDROP. THE BIRDCAGE MAKES AN UNUSUAL CENTERPIECE.

△

ABOVE RIGHT FALLS OF HEAVY SILK BEHIND A DINING TABLE, WITH SHEERS BEHIND, ACHIEVE A THEATRICAL EFFECT THAT IS UNDERLINED BY THE MATCHING HORSE SCULPTURES. THE FOUNTAIN-LIKE FLOW OF THE CURTAINS, OBTAINED BY CATCHING EACH ONE TWICE WITH CIRCULAR CORDS, IS ACCENTUATED BY THE CRYSTAL DROPS OF THE CHANDELIER. THREE SWAGS ALTERNATING WITH FOUR TAILS COMPLETE THE EFFECT.

▷

SIMPLE CURTAINS IN GOLDEN COTTON WITH A SUBDUED BRAID TRIM ARE GIVEN A TOUCH OF EXCITEMENT BY A SURMOUNTING VALANCE, HEAVILY FESTOONED, BENEATH A CORNICE IN CONTRASTING BLACK AND GOLD.

An interesting feature of this arrangement is the unusually shaped cushioned cornice, covered with self-striped velour. From this falls a pair of full, plain curtains. Notice the use of mirror panels between, around and below the sash windows. The overall effect is simple yet dramatic.

This "Neo-Grecian" arrangement creates a highly theatrical look. At the top, beneath a cornice decorated with Greek motifs, a complex valance animated by mythical creatures hangs from a molded cornice decorated with lions. The outer dress curtains are bordered with a Greek key motif and caught by fan-shaped brackets. Then comes a plain tasseled inner curtain, asymmetrically arranged, and as a final layer an opaque shade with decorative base.

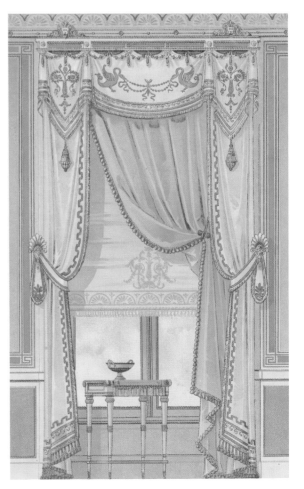

In an age of standardization, it is all the more important for us to express individuality in our homes. In curtaining, as in other aspects of design, the precise balance of novelty and tradition is a matter for individual taste. You can take an established style and give it a special character by varying an expected aspect of it – perhaps the shape, fabric or decorative trimmings. Or, if you prefer a bolder statement, you can allow your imagination even more freedom, discarding conventional solutions. The fireplace arrangements on this page show this degree of originality: avoiding the predictable, they each give a highly individual stamp to the room that contains them.

Anyone apprehensive about making grand gestures of this sort can take comfort from historical precedents. Catherine de Medici startled 16th-century Italian courtiers with a black velvet bed cover embroidered all over with pearls. A notable mold-breaker of our own times was the Virginia-born designer Nancy Lancaster, who combined old and new fabrics, painted designs on top of plain materials, and appliquéed unlikely frgments of textiles on to plain backgrounds. By breaking the rules in this way, you can create imaginative effects.

Part of the secret is to avoid the obvious. Instead of selecting trimmings from your local curtain shop, consider dressmaker's trimmings – ribbons in your favorite colors plaited together; starched broderie anglaise used for a tie-back on a lightweight curtain; rows of wavy rick-rack braid stitched along the edge to make borders; or flower-printed lawn bordering yards of muslin. Flea markets, junk shops and auction rooms can be a rich source of unusual textiles and trimmings. Look out for antique curtains in good condition, as these can often be cut down or otherwise altered to make an individual arrangement.

Experiment with unusual color combinations – such as dark blue with terracotta, purple with pink, or dazzling black and white. Bear in mind too the possibility of dyeing fabrics: raw silks, when dyed, will sing with color.

No one is saying that it is easy to be an individualist. It requires forethought and, above all, confidence. Not everyone will applaud what you have done, but at least you will have the satisfaction of having created a room in your own unique style.

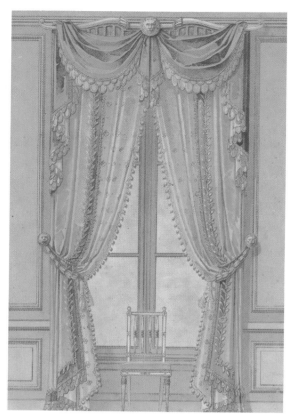

◁

A UNIQUE EMPIRE-STYLE ARRANGEMENT WITH DISTINCTIVE BORDERS OF OVERLAPPING SCALES. THE BOW-SHAPED POLE HOLDS UP SILK SWAGS AND TAILS. BELOW THIS, THE OUTER CURTAINS HAVE AN INNER BAND OF DEEPER COLOR, EDGED WITH APPLIQUÉ LEAVES AND BRAIDING. THE INNER CURTAINS, ALSO IN SILK, ARE SCATTERED WITH FLOWERS. THE LION'S HEAD ON THE BOW IS MATCHED BY SMALLER HEADS ON THE BRACKETS WHICH HOLD THE TIE-BACKS.

▷

FIREPLACES ARE NOT NORMALLY DRESSED WITH FABRIC, BUT THE TWO EXAMPLES HERE SHOW HOW YOU CAN BREAK THE RULES TO SUPERB EFFECT. THE LARGE PICTURE (RIGHT) SHOWS DRAMATIC USE OF SOFT WHITE SILK AROUND AN OVERMANTEL MIRROR. INSTEAD OF BEING HELD DOWN BY BATTENS AS USUAL, THE DRAPES ARE ALLOWED TO FALL CASUALLY TO THE FLOOR.

▽

THE SAME CONCEPT, BUT WITHOUT THE LOOSE, FESTOONED EFFECT: THE FABRIC IS FIRMLY STRETCHED ACROSS THE WALLS, EXCEPT WHERE IT IS PARTED BY THE FIREPLACE AND AT THE WINDOWS TO FORM DRAPES. A WIDE BORDER ADDS INTEREST AT CORNICE LEVEL. NOTE THE MATCHING FABRIC IN PLEATS WITHIN AND BELOW THE ALCOVES.

THE MOST DISTINCTIVE FEATURE OF THIS LOUIS XVI WINDOW DRESSING IS THE CORNICE DECORATION OF GARLANDS, BOWS AND RIBBONS, REDOLENT OF MARIE ANTOINETTE, AND THE ECHOING SWAGS CAUGHT WITH SOFT BOWS. THE TAILS ARE LIFTED TO THE TOP OF THE CORNICE BEFORE BEING ALLOWED TO FALL AT EITHER SIDE.

◁

DESIGNER NINA CAMPBELL HAS STRIKINGLY DRESSED THIS BAY WITH FOUR CURTAINS, FIXED AT CORNICE LEVEL, AND CAUGHT HALF-WAY DOWN THE WINDOW AND AGAIN AT DADO LEVEL. A DIAPHANOUS PRINTED AUSTRIAN SHADE SITS BELOW. AS THERE IS NO VALANCE, A DECORATIVE BAND OF FABRIC HIDES THE ROD.

▷

EXTRAVAGANTLY SCULPTURAL, THIS PAIR OF CREAM SILK CURTAINS IS SET OFF BY A NARROW SWAG CAUGHT BY A BOW AT EACH SIDE, WITH A CENTRAL BOW FOR GOOD MEASURE. THE CURTAINS ARE CAUGHT IN TWO FAT FURBELOWS, AND THEN FALL LOOSELY TO THE FLOOR. AGAINST THE WINDOW IS A WHITE COTTON LACE CURTAIN.

◁

A GOOD EXAMPLE OF THE STRIKING EFFECTS THAT CAN BE ACHIEVED BY USING MANY METERS OF AN INEXPENSIVE FABRIC. HERE, MUSLIN HAS BEEN DYED AND USED WITH ABANDON IN A MOST ORIGINAL WAY — LOOPS AND CURVES FORMING SWAGS AND TAILS, AND EVEN CATCHING UP THE MAIN CURTAINS IN A FINAL TOUCH OF BRAVADO. KNOTTING THE FABRIC NEAR FLOOR LEVEL HAS ADDED DECORATIVE FLOURISHES. THE ARRANGEMENT IS BROADLY, BUT NOT STRICTLY, SYMMETRICAL.

◁

THE APPARENTLY CASUAL LOOK OF THESE HEAVY RAW SILK CURTAINS IS IN FACT THE RESULT OF CAREFUL CONTRIVANCE. THE VALANCE, WHICH SWEEPS DOWN TO FORM TAILS, HAS BEEN CUT TO LOOK AS IF ONE HALF OF THE FABRIC HAS SIMPLY BEEN THROWN OVER THE OTHER. THE FRINGING HAS BEEN DESIGNED TO BE HALF-HIDDEN, AS HAVE THE TASSELS GLIMPSED THROUGH THE TAILS. BELOW THIS ELABORATE ARTIFICE, THE CURTAINS ARE ALLOWED TO HANG NATURALLY TO FLOOR LEVEL.

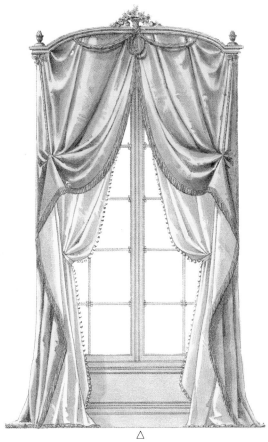

PLAIN COLORS CAN BE USED TO SIMPLE YET
SUMPTUOUS EFFECT, AS IN THIS LOUIS XVI
TREATMENT. ALTHOUGH THE VALANCE IS
ELABORATE, THE CURTAINS ARE ARRANGED WITH
RESTRAINT — THE OUTER BLUE PAIR HELD UP BY
CORDS TO SHOW ITS COMPLEMENTARY YELLOW
LINING, THE INNER PINK PAIR BY TIE-BACKS.

▷

TO SIMPLIFY THE TREATMENT OF A PAIR OF
WINDOWS CLOSE TOGETHER, YOU CAN APPROACH
THE COMPOSITION AS ONE WINDOW. HERE,
COTTON CHINTZ CASE-HEADED ON A POLE FRAMES
INNER CURTAINS OF STRIPED VOILE, WHICH
MATCHES THE LININGS AND BORDERS OF THE
OUTER CURTAINS.

▷▷

A SINGLE CURTAIN IN SUBDUED STRIPES, CASE-
HEADED ON A BRASS POLE WITH FINIALS AND
CAUGHT BY A BRASS ACANTHUS LEAF BRACKET,
DECORATES A SMALL WINDOW. THE BORDER HAS
THE SAME STRIPES, BUT ON A SLANT.

The simple approach to curtaining is often the most successful. It is not a new concept, but one that has enjoyed favor at various times in the past. Although there have been phases when it became virtually impossible to look out of a window, pass through a door or climb into a bed without encountering voluminous furbelows of fabric, there have been periods too when reticence was the rule. For the Georgians, for example, simplicity was the most sought-after of virtues. Even today, for some people, simplicity of design has acquired almost philosophical overtones, as a deliberate statement of rebellion against frivolity and the costs of conspicuous consumption.

Simplicity need not imply unwelcoming austerity: rather, the confidence to let the fabric speak for itself, uncluttered by decorative details. Such a treatment may be particularly appropriate in rooms where hard-edged furniture dominates. It may also be suitable where the furniture, for whatever reason, is so special that it warrants an undistracting setting.

A restrained treatment of fabrics can work as well in a very formal room as in a more humble interior. When opulence is the keynote, simple

AN ORIGINAL TREATMENT OF MATCHING CURTAINS AND BLINDS IN STRIPED COTTON TICKING. THE CURTAINS, CASE-HEADED ONTO A POLE WITH A RUFF ABOVE, ARE SECURED AT THE CENTER AND CAUGHT BACK WITH TIE-BACKS IN THE SAME FABRIC: THESE ARE PLACED UNUSUALLY HIGH. THE ROMAN SHADE BEHIND PROVIDES INSULATION AND ALLOWS CAREFUL CONTROL OF LIGHT.

▷
ORGANZA CURTAINS HUNG FROM A CLASSIC BRASS POLE OF SMALL DIAMETER CREATE A STRIKING IMPACT. THE UNUSUAL COMBINATION OF BURGUNDY FABRIC AND BRIGHT PINK WALLS AND SOFA IS A RISK THAT WORKS TRIUMPHANTLY.

curtains can add a breath of fresh air to a scene that could otherwise become somewhat overpowering.

Paradoxically, keeping things simple is not always a simple matter. It is often harder to get simple curtains to look right than elaborate ones. Because there will be no frills, swags or complicated headings to divert the eye, special attention has to be paid to scale and line.

Silk and velvet can look superb in the right environment, but so can less expensive fabrics such as ticking, unbleached cotton or plain sheers. When making your choice, bear in mind the mood you want to create. Color, of course, will be just as important a factor as fabric. If you

are considering bold, arresting colors, first ask yourself whether they might not begin to feel psychologically uncomfortable with prolonged exposure. For a room designed for relaxation, a better choice might be neutral colors in an interesting weave, or perhaps a low-key color trimmed in simple style with a contrasting shade.

Large-scale patterns that look bold and simple in the shop may appear disappointingly complicated when you hang them in their intended position at your window. However, if you choose with care, taking the folds into account, a formalized pattern of geometrical shapes, or perhaps stylized plant or flower motifs, can make a simple statement that will

inject a dash of life into your room without being too unsettling.

The very essence of simplicity is the flat surface presented by a roller shade, but this might be just a little *too* philosophical for some people. Roller shades or flat-pleated Roman shades in association with curtains are perhaps a more popular option: they look particularly effective when both components are in white or cream.

A simple window treatment is usually the best, if only as an interim measure, in a room where you find yourself unable to come to a firm decision about a coherent design. Not least of the virtues of simplicity are that it is easy to live with – and easy to change.

THIS TRADITIONAL ARRANGEMENT CONSISTS OF
NOTHING MORE THAN HEAVY STRIPED SILK
CURTAINS HUNG FROM RINGS ON A POLE, AND A
PLAIN ROLLER SHADE AGAINST THE WINDOW. THE
CURTAIN HEADING HAS BEEN TIGHTLY PULLED TO
GIVE A PRETTY BUNCHED EFFECT. THE POLE AND
RINGS ARE PAINTED IN PALE GRAY TO MATCH THE
REST OF THE WOODWORK.

△

THIS SIMPLE TREATMENT OF A BAY
COMBINES CURTAINS AND NARROW-
SLATTED VENETIAN BLINDS. THE
SINGLE CURTAINS ARE IN HEAVY
CREAM COTTON EDGED AND BANDED
WITH CHECKED BORDERS, WITH A
FRENCH-PLEATED HEADING.

◁

A HISTORIC TREATMENT FOR A
PORTIÈRE, USING JUST TWO PIECES
OF PLAIN FABRIC. ONE CURTAIN
HANGS STRAIGHT, WHILE THE OTHER,
DRAWN ACROSS IT, IS HELD BY FLEUR-
DE-LYS BRACKETS ON A SERIES OF
CORDS AND RINGS. PULLING THE
LONG CORD AT THE RIGHT (JUST
VISIBLE) LIFTS THE CURTAIN TO
ALLOW ACCESS.

△

IN A ROOM WITH AN ELABORATE BED
TREATMENT, THE CURTAINS NEED TO
BE RELATIVELY RESTRAINED. THIS
CURVED BAY HAS FOUR CURTAINS AT
THE WINDOW DIVISIONS, EACH ONE
TIED BACK AT SILL LEVEL. A THIN
BAND OF CONTRASTING FABRIC
ABOVE THE FRENCH-PLEATED
HEADING PROVIDES DEFINITION. THE
SHADES BEHIND MATCH THE BED.

▷

THE GRAPHIC BEDROOM TREATMENT
ABOVE IS ECHOED HERE IN THE
DINING ROOM OF THE SAME HOUSE.
THE ONLY DIFFERENCE IN THE
CURTAINS IS THE USE OF A BROWN
TRIM AROUND THE EDGES INSTEAD OF
BLUE-GRAY. THE SAME BROWN TRIM
IS USED TO DECORATE THE BASE OF
THE OTHERWISE PLAIN ROLLER
SHADE.

▷

SOFT, DEEP VALANCES CREATE A MOOD OF RELAXED LUXURY, SUITABLE FOR HOMES IN BOTH TOWN AND COUNTRY. THIS 19TH-CENTURY WINDOW TREATMENT IS GRAND, BUT ITS AMBIENCE IS NONETHELESS WARM AND WELCOMING. THE FLOWERED CRETONNE CURTAINS HANG FROM A DEEP BOX-PLEATED VALANCE IN THE SAME FABRIC.

◁

THIS TREATMENT IS MORE ELABORATE THAN THE ONE ALONGSIDE (FAR LEFT), AND HAS A STIFFENED FABRIC-COVERED CORNICE INSTEAD OF A SOFT VALANCE. HOWEVER, THE EFFECT REMAINS ONE OF CHARM AND FRESHNESS RATHER THAN STIFF FORMALITY. THE INNER LACE CURTAINS ARE UNUSUAL IN HAVING THEIR OWN CURVING SWAG.

For some people, the countryside is the landscape all around, the view that their windows frame. For others, country living is a state of mind, an idealized world that can be pleasantly evoked in a town house or city apartment, by careful choice of wall coverings and window treatments. The rooms illustrated here and on the following four pages, mostly in town houses or grander country homes, all capture a soft, fresh, welcoming mood with distinct overtones of the outdoors.

In urban homes, country furniture often looks absurdly out of place rather than nostalgically evocative – as if the owners were trying to pull a grand confidence trick on gullible visitors. Curtains – fresh, bright and simple – offer a more subtle, and usually more successful, way to conjure up the open air, especially when combined with polished floors, warm-toned rugs and carpets, and bowls of fresh flowers in every room.

To conjure up a traditional country home, the most important ingredient is the fabric, and more specifically the pattern. Flowers are the most potent symbol of the countryside, and we are fortunate today in having a wide range of floral patterns to choose from. Old chintzes have been painstakingly reproduced, and there is also a generous repertoire of new chintzes from designers all over the world. Both reproduction and modern flower curtains are available in appropriately soft colors with unashamedly pretty designs that are redolent of the country garden. You can mix the patterns in a room, using them for chair covers and tablecloths as well as for curtains – with the proviso that they should share the same range of tones.

Of course, plain colors also have their charm. You need not confine yourself to pastel and pale: clear, bright colors can work just as well, so long as they do not clash with other features.

Tradition should also be reflected in the shape of the curtains. Whether they are long or short, the best policy is usually to keep them simple. A valance or simple swags might be considered, and you can certainly use luxurious fabrics; however, gold fringing and tassels would spoil the freshness of the arrangement.

◁

OAK PANELING WITH EXUBERANT CHINTZ CURTAINS SPELL A COUNTRY HOUSE LOOK, EVEN THOUGH THE SETTING IS URBAN. THE VALANCES ARE DEEP AND SOFT, WITH A DEEP GREEN BORDER THAT DEFINES THEIR SHAPE. THE SAME BORDER EDGES THE CURTAINS, WHICH ARE TIED BACK WITH ROPES IN MATCHING GREEN.

◁◁

IN AN UPPER ROOM THAT OVERLOOKS A PARK, GARDEN SQUARE OR STRETCH OF COUNTRYSIDE, YOU CAN AFFORD TO TAKE A MINIMAL APPROACH TO THE WINDOW DRESSINGS. HERE, THE ONLY FABRIC USED IS SOFT, SHEER, FRINGED MUSLIN DRAPED INTO A SIMPLE TAILED SWAG SET INSIDE EACH WINDOW FRAME. THE SUBTLE PAINT COLOR AND DELICATE WALLPAPER REINFORCE THE SOFTNESS OF THE MOOD.

COUNTRY FRESHNESS

◁

THE RICH GREEN OF THIS LOUIS XVI ARRANGEMENT WOULD BE A CLASSIC CHOICE FOR A GRAND COUNTRY HOUSE — ESPECIALLY A LUXURIOUS LIBRARY, LINED FROM FLOOR TO CEILING WITH LEATHER-BOUND BOOKS, WHERE THE RESTFUL ATMOSPHERE OF GREEN WOULD CREATE A SUITABLE AMBIENCE. THE COMPLEX CORNICE, WITH SCALLOPS, BRAIDING AND TASSELS, CROWNS TWO LAYERS OF CURTAINS BACKED BY A RUCHED SILK AUSTRIAN SHADE.

▽

BELOW LEFT RED ROSES ON CHINTZ CURTAINS AND MATCHING CUSHIONS BRING A FRESH, ROMANTIC LOOK TO THIS INTIMATE ROOM CROWDED WITH FINE PAINTINGS. THE DEEP GOBLET-PLEATED VALANCE IS FRINGED IN AN ATTRACTIVE BLUE THAT PICKS OUT THE LEAF COLOR IN THE PATTERN. THE CURTAINS THEMSELVES ARE TREATED SIMPLY, LETTING THE PATTERN MAKE ITS OWN STATEMENT, WITH BROAD TIE-BACKS CAMOUFLAGED BY THE USE OF THE SAME FABRIC.

▷

ONLY A SMALL ROOM WITH RELATIVELY LITTLE FURNITURE CAN TAKE THIS MUCH PATTERN. THE WALLS, SOFA, CHAIR AND CURTAINS ALL SHARE THE SAME FLOWERY FABRIC. NOTICE THE DEEP INDENTS IN THE VALANCE AND THE WAY IN WHICH THE NARROW RED TRIM EDGING THE CURTAINS, VALANCE AND TIE-BACKS LINKS UP WITH A SIMILAR TRIM AROUND THE WALLS.

▽

THE TONE IN THIS COUNTRIFIED BEDROOM IS SET BY THE CONTRAST OF A FRESH FLORAL PATTERN AGAINST A CREAMY BACKGROUND. THE PATTERN IS PRESENTED AS FOUR DIFFERENT ELEMENTS, EACH MAKING APPROXIMATELY THE SAME VISUAL IMPACT — THE INNER CURTAIN ABOVE THE BEDHEAD, THE VALANCE OF THE BED, THE SCALLOPED SHADE AND THE ARMCHAIR. THE AREAS OF PLAIN FABRIC ARE UNIFIED BY A DELICATE RED TRIM. TO ADD TO THE RURAL MOOD AND BRING THE PATTERNS TO LIFE, A BASKET OF FLOWERS HAS BEEN CASUALLY PLACED ON THE CARPET.

COUNTRY FRESHNESS

▷
TWO BUSY PAISLEY PATTERNS FORM THE
THEMATIC LINK BETWEEN CURTAINS AND WALL IN
THIS HOMELY LIVING ROOM. THE GOBLET HEADING
IS IN THE SAME PATTERN AS THE LINING.

▷▷
A FLORAL COMPOSITION IN FABRIC AND
WALLPAPER TELLS A STORY OF THE COUNTRYSIDE.
AS WITH MANY OF THE OTHER FLOWER PATTERNS
SHOWN IN THIS SECTION, THE CURTAINS HAVE
BEEN KEPT RELATIVELY SIMPLE.

▽
YELLOW USED IN A PATTERN WITH A BLUE STRIPE
AND LITTLE WHITE FLOWERS CREATES A SUNNY,
OPEN-AIR MOOD IN THIS BEDROOM. THE CURTAINS
HAVE BEEN SMOCKED INTO A WIDE PLEATED
HEADING, AND THE TIE-BACKS ARE SCALLOPED.

WHEN THE OUTER CURTAINS ARE RELATIVELY ELABORATE, YOU MIGHT WANT TO MAKE THE INNER SHEERS SUITABLY ORNAMENTAL TOO. DECORATIVE BORDERS LIKE THOSE IN THIS 19TH-CENTURY ARRANGEMENT WILL LOOK IMPRESSIVE WHEN THE SUN SHINES THROUGH AND PICKS OUT THE MOTIFS.

SHEERS ARE EASY TO MANIPULATE, AND CAN BE CONTRIVED WITHOUT DIFFICULTY TO FIT THE SHAPE OF AN ARCHED WINDOW LIKE THIS ONE IN A LIVING ROOM. THE WHITE MUSLIN CURTAIN ON ITS SPECIALLY BUILT, TIGHT-FITTING FRAME IS HELD BACK INVISIBLY, AS IF BY A BREEZE, SO THAT THE LIGHT ENTERING THE ROOM IS PARTLY DIRECT, PARTLY DIFFUSED.

Sheer curtains admit natural light into a room. However, they have often been considered to be in distinctly bad taste. Edith Wharton, the American novelist, in her book *The Decoration of Houses* (1897), was dismissive of muslin. While agreeing that muslin might have a practical use with the new, large sheet-glass windows, she notes with disdain: "Lingerie effects do not commune well with architecture."

When the swings of fabric fashion put muslin back in favor, it was the turn of the lace curtain to be shunned. In 1910 one commentator, Elsie de Wolfe, thundered: "I hope it is not necessary for me to go into the matter of lace curtains here. I feel sure that no woman of really good taste could prefer a cheap curtain of imitation lace to a simple one of white muslin."

Today, lightweight, see-through curtains are in favour again – not only lace and muslins, but silks and gauze, voiles, cheesecloth and the whole range of synthetic translucents. The variety of see-through fabrics available offers all kinds of possibilities in any room of the house, from the grandest and most formal of drawing rooms to the smallest, simplest bathrooms. Sheers can look especially pretty as bed curtains, on a half-canopy or a four-poster, or simply defining a bed set into an alcove or corner.

There are many synthetic sheers, some better-looking than others. Almost all are easier to care

for than natural fabrics (at windows, sheers are the first defense against dust and dirt, and thus need frequent washing, especially in towns). They also tend to keep their color longer. Look for fabrics that are heavy enough to hang well.

See-through curtains do not have to be in white. Muslins and laces come also in shades of cream and buttermilk, and other sheers are available in a variety of soft colors.

Whatever the fabric, sheers demand a delicate touch. They can be used on their own or in conjunction with heavier curtains. You could try accompanying them with swags and tails of a completely different material, or with another sheer fabric of different weight. Sheers can be swagged, draped and looped, formally cut and sewn, or turned artlessly over a pole.

When calculating the amount of material for sheer curtaining, usually you will need more than you think, so that the fabric can fall in fine folds or hang loosely in billows. Many sheers sold by the yard or meter come in larger widths than usual, avoiding the need for an ugly seam that would stand out against the light. Take this into account when using sheers as a pair: measure and hang them with care so that they do not overlap to show a darker central strip where they meet. When a sheer fabric is used alone at a tall window, weight the base of the curtain with weighted tape so that it sits well.

A FINE FIGURED LACE PANEL WITH A BEAUTIFUL FLORAL DESIGN GIVES PRIVACY IN THIS BATHROOM, AND ELIMINATES GLARE. HERE, FOR MAXIMUM CONTROL OVER THE LIGHT, THE PANEL IS USED AS A ROLLER SHADE, BUT IT COULD EQUALLY WELL HAVE BEEN USED AS A FLAT, FIXED SURFACE.

ALTHOUGH NOT STRICTLY SHEER, THIS LUSH BALLOON-SHADE IN NATURAL STRIPED SILK NOT ONLY MATCHES THE UPHOLSTERY BUT HAS A TRANSLUCENCY AND AIRINESS THAT GO WELL WITH THE CHARACTER OF THE ROOM. PLAIN SHEER PANELS BEHIND PRESENT A SOLID WALL OF LIGHT.

▽

A THOROUGHLY MODERN INTERPRETATION OF THE MEDIEVAL FASHION FOR BED HANGINGS. THE OBVIOUS WAY TO GIVE A LIGHT, SUMMERY ENCLOSURE TO THIS BED WOULD HAVE BEEN WITH AN ENVELOPE OF SHEERS. THIS TREATMENT IS MORE ORIGINAL — A SIMPLE SELF-STRIPED COTTON SURROUND AT THE HEAD, MATCHED AT THE FOOT BY L-SHAPED PILLARS, ALL HANGING FROM THE CEILING IN DEEP FOLDS. THE MOOD CREATED IS ONE OF PRIVACY WITHOUT CLAUSTROPHOBIA.

△

A PAIR OF HEAVY SHEER CURTAINS IN DEEP LUSCIOUS FOLDS SWEEPING DOWN TO FLOOR LEVEL IS USED HERE TO GIVE A SENSE OF ENCLOSURE TO AN UNUSUAL STAIRCASE LANDING WITH A CURVED BALUSTRADE. THE ELABORATE WOODEN POLE, MOLDED, GILDED AND PICKED OUT WITH MOTIFS IN BLACK, CLEVERLY HIDES THE ROD. AT THE SIDES THE CURTAINS ARE TIED WITH SIMPLE ROPES AND TASSELS.

◁

CREAMY, LINED, LACE CURTAINS AT THE WINDOW OF THIS BEDROOM, PULLED BACK INVISIBLY DURING THE DAY, HARMONIZE WITH THE LACE BED HANGINGS. THE WALLPAPER, PAINTWORK AND CARPET ALL WORK WITH THE FABRICS TO MAKE A LIGHT BACKGROUND AGAINST WHICH RED MOTIFS STAND OUT VIVIDLY.

◁

FIGURED COTTON LACE CURTAINS MAKE THIS DARK ROOM SEEM LIGHTER, AND CONTRAST WITH ORNATE GOLD MOLDINGS ON THE PICTURES AND MIRROR. THEY FALL FROM A GILDED CORNICE AND ARE CAUGHT AT THE BASE OF THE WINDOW.

▷

LIGHT CURTAINS DO NOT NECESSARILY HAVE TO BE FLOOR-LENGTH. IN THIS BEDROOM, THE SHEERS ARE GESTURES RATHER THAN FULL-SCALE STATEMENTS. THE HEADING IS CASE-HEADED ONTO A NARROW POLE, AND THERE ARE TIES THREE-QUARTERS OF THE WAY DOWN THE WINDOW. THE DELICACY OF THESE CURTAINS COMPLEMENTS THE WALL DECORATION AT CEILING LEVEL.

▽

THE INTEREST HERE LIES IN THE STRIKING CONTRAST BETWEEN THE SIMPLICITY OF THE COTTON LACE CURTAINS AND THE FORMALITY OF THE DECORATED WINDOW SURROUND. THE DEEP VALANCE HAS A FRILL, REPEATED ALONG THE CURTAIN EDGES AND ON THE TIE-BACKS.

△

CURTAINING FOR A WINDOW NEEDS TO TAKE INTO ACCOUNT SHAPE AND PROPORTION. THIS FULL-LENGTH WINDOW WITH A PATTERNED STRUCTURE HAS BEEN GIVEN A TREATMENT APPROPRIATE TO ITS IMPORTANCE. TODAY THE WINDOW WOULD BE TREATED MUCH LESS ELABORATELY, BUT THE BASIC SHAPE OF THIS TREATMENT IS TIMELESSLY APT AND WOULD WORK EQUALLY WELL WITH SIMPLIFIED TRIMMINGS.

▷

SOME WINDOWS HAVE AN INHERENT BEAUTY THAT YOU MUST BE CAREFUL NOT TO OBSCURE WITH FABRIC. THIS IS A VENETIAN (OR PALLADIAN) WINDOW — A CENTRAL ROUND-HEADED ARCH WITH A RECTANGULAR SECTION AT EITHER SIDE. TO MAKE THE MOST OF THIS, A SIMPLE, PLAIN DRESSING HAS BEEN DEVISED, WITH A CURVED HEADING ON THE CENTRAL CURTAIN THAT FITS THE SHAPE OF THE ARCH.

Tall, relatively narrow windows are a hallmark of Georgian architecture. Elegant, light-giving and pleasing in their proportions, they are coveted even by those who in other aspects of the home favor a more modern style. In particular, they are associated with the first-floor room of the 18th- and early 19th-century town house – the *piano nobile*. Anyone lucky enough to have a home of this design, or based on this design, has an opportunity for superb window treatments.

Historic paintings and prints show Austrian shades employed to filter the light and decorate tall windows without detracting from their architectural lines. However, in modern times the Austrian shade has suffered many indignaties—accretions of frills, ruffles and bows, often added with complete disregard for the shape of the window or the design of the fabric. Such overdressing should be avoided at all costs.

However, an Austrian shade that allows the fabric to speak for itself, set against a tall window with fine reveals, can look stunning.

Other simple hanging styles will also flatter the tall classic window. The options include a flat Roman shade that shows off the frame; a pair of curtains in a plain fabric with a simple swag draped over a pole above; a single curtain, caught diagonally across the frame; or a generous swathe of muslin to diffuse the light, falling naturally into folds on the floor. Curtains for tall windows can be hung at architrave level, or fixed above the architrave so that the cornice over the window is hidden by the curtain heading. This latter treatment is ill-advised with an antique plaster cornice, but can make a dramatic effect when the plaster surround is undistinguished.

If the proportions of the window are correct, the controlling principle for both simple and

△

A TALL WINDOW CAN TAKE AN ORNATE CORNICE OR VALANCE WITHOUT THE EFFECT BECOMING TOP-HEAVY. THIS LOUIS XV DESIGN HAS A CARVED WOODEN MOLDING FROM WHICH HANGS A FABRIC-COVERED FRINGED CORNICE WITH A PANEL OF EMBROIDERED SILK. OUTER CURTAINS IN DARK GREEN SILK ARE EDGED WITH NARROW GOLD FRINGING AND TIED BACK TO SHOW A PINK LINING. THE INNER CURTAINS ARE IN THE SAME FABRIC AS THE VALANCE PANEL.

▷

THESE BEAUTIFUL SASH WINDOWS IN NATURAL WOOD, WITH FINE MOLDINGS, RECEIVE FABRIC DRESSINGS THAT ARE EQUALLY LUXURIOUS, WITH SWAGS, TAILS AND ROSETTES, IN A MUTED BUT DISTINCTIVE TWO-TONE COLOR SCHEME. THE BOBBLED FRINGES IN THE MAIN FABRIC COLOR STAND OUT BEAUTIFULLY AGAINST BROAD BANDS OF CONTRASTING GRAY, ADDING LIVELINESS TO THE OVERALL DESIGN. THE TIE-BACKS, ALSO IN GRAY, ARE POSITIONED LOW, EMPHASIZING THE WINDOWS' HEIGHT.

complex window hangings is to keep them so. Carry the mathematics of the window frame through to the fabric treatment. Avoid top-heavy valances and curtains that skimp on fabric. Use plenty of material, or the look of easy grace that is so important to these windows will be entirely lost.

Unfortunately, many tall windows fail to conform to Georgian rules of proportion, and in such cases the curtaining treatment is more problematic. Classically, the architrave at the top of the window should be at picture rail level, allowing an area of wall space between the window and the ceiling or cornice. This rule is often broken. In many converted houses, the ceiling has been lowered, so that the window finishes high up against it. This is also the situation in some modern homes. Where this difficulty occurs, the valances or drapes must be

designed so that they bring the eye down, away from the top of the window. Long, elegant tails, or a valance that curves to a lower point at each side, would have this effect. If the curtains are to be tied back, the tie should be relatively low to achieve the best effect.

You can hang tall curtains at architrave level, or fix them higher so that the heading hides the cornice above the window. Although the latter treatment is not advisable if you have an old or attractive plaster cornice, it can enhance a hitherto undistinguished surround.

Not all tall windows are floor-length. Often, although they rise to the top of the room, they finish a considerable distance above the floor. Even if a radiator or a piece of furniture is placed in the space beneath, such windows should be treated as if they went to the floor or baseboard level, with full-length curtains.

△

AN EMPIRE-STYLE STOOL IN FRONT OF A FULL-LENGTH WINDOW IS FRAMED BY A GENEROUSLY FESTOONED BALLOON SHADE, SHEERS BEHIND, AND A ROLLER SHADE AGAINST THE WINDOW. THE RED COLOR ACCENTS MAKE A SUBTLE IMPACT.

◁

FLORAL CURTAINS HUNG FROM A CURVED ROD REACH FROM FLOOR TO CEILING AND FILL ALMOST THE WHOLE WIDTH OF THE HALL. AT THE BOTTOM THEY ARE SLANTED TO MAKE FRINGED TAILS. THE FRINGES ECHO THE KNOTTED CORDS AND TASSELS AT THE FLEMISH HEADING, AS WELL AS THE CORD TIE-BACKS. THE ROLLER SHADE MATCHES THE WALLS.

◁◁

CENTER FOLLOWING A 19TH-CENTURY FASHION, SWAGS FALL FROM A CENTRAL ROSETTE HIGH AGAINST THE CEILING. ALL THE ROSETTES ARE IN A SUBTLY PATTERNED FABRIC. THE HIGH FOCAL POINT IS EMPHASIZED BY TASSELS, REVEALED BY A NARROW PARTING BETWEEN THE DRAPES. LOOSE DOUBLE TWISTED CORDS FORM THE TIE-BACKS.

◁

TALL WINDOWS DO NOT ALWAYS NEED
CURTAINS OR SHADES TO SHOW THEM
OFF TO BEST ADVANTAGE. HERE,
SWAGS AND MATCHING TAILS,
BACKED BY A PLEATED VALANCE, MAKE
AN EFFECTIVE STATEMENT ON THEIR
OWN. THE BRACKET CLOCK BETWEEN
THE WINDOWS IS APPROPRIATELY
ORNATE, BALANCING THE FABRIC
TREATMENT. FLOWERS AND TABLE
LAMPS REINFORCE THE SYMMETRY.

△

FULL-LENGTH FRENCH-PLEATED CURTAINS IN
SUMPTUOUS DEEP BROWN HANG FROM THE
BOTTOM LINE OF A ANCANTHUS-LEAF PLASTER
CORNICE. THE CURTAIN COLOR TONES WELL WITH
CARPET, UPHOLSTERY, TABLECLOTH AND CUSHIONS.

◁

AN IMPRESSIVE ARRANGEMENT IN RICH GOLDEN
COLOURS. ABOVE EACH OF THE TWO WINDOWS,
THE FLAT CORNICE COVERED IN STRIPED SILK IS THE
BACKGROUND FOR A SWAG MADE IN ONE PIECE OF
FABRIC BUT DRESSED TO FORM TWO FESTOONS, A
TAIL-LIKE EFFECT IN THE CENTER AND LONG TAILS
AT EITHER SIDE. FRINGING, BUNCHED ROSETTES
AND A LINING IN DEEP GOLDEN BROWN COMPLETE
THE EFFECT. THE CURTAINS THEMSELVES ARE
SIMPLE AND STRAIGHT.

▷

THE TOPS OF THESE FRENCH-PLEATED CURTAINS
IN CHEERFUL STRIPES ARE HIDDEN BEHIND A
PLAIN ARCHITECTURAL CORNICE WHICH RUNS THE
WHOLE LENGTH OF THE WALL AND THUS MAKES
THE TWO WINDOWS APPEAR AS ONE. THE ONLY
DECORATIVE EXTRAS ARE WAVY FRINGES IN THE
SAME STRIPES AND LOOSELY TWISTED DOUBLE-
CORD TIE-BACKS. THE SOFA IS PLACED OFF-
CENTER TO AVOID TOO STATIC AN IMPRESSION.

△

A CHIC PARISIAN TREATMENT SHOWS
A SCALLOPED, FLOWERED CORNICE
FALLING FROM A PLAIN MOLDING.
THE OUTER CURTAINS IN THE SAME
PATTERN ARE SIMPLY FRINGED AND
TIED BACK WITH CORDS AND TASSELS
ONTO CLASSICAL BRACKETS.
RECTANGULAR LACE PANELS
COVERING THE WINDOWS
THEMSELVES ARE DESIGNED TO
DIFFUSE THE LIGHT ATTRACTIVELY.
THIS HISTORIC TREATMENT COULD
EASILY BE IMITATED TODAY.

The 1950s and 60s saw the culmination of the tendency for windows to become gradually larger. This was the heyday of the picture window – one enormous pane of glass, often extending to the floor, and designed to encompass the world outside, making it seem almost part of the room.

At its best, the picture window is a striking feature and needs little embellishment. Unfortunately, though, many picture windows today show a picture of other peoples' lives – and privacy becomes more of a priority than the view.

Whatever the outlook, such a large window can be difficult to curtain successfully without the results looking like a set of stage curtains. Practically speaking, too, a window that lets in as much light as this can also let in an unwanted degree of cold air, a single sheet of glass not being the best of insulators. Storm windows are, of course, one answer. However, suitable solutions can also be found with curtains.

Obviously, only full-length curtains should be used on a window that extends to the floor. These should be lined and interlined to make them hang well and to improve their insulating qualities. They should extend, wherever possible, beyond the sides of the window frame, to cut out edges of cold air. However, curtains need not be full-length where there is a sill to break their fall.

If there is a sliding door incorporated into the window, the curtains should extend back as far as possible to allow access, and the pole or rod should be fixed high enough to allow the curtains and sliding door to operate smoothly and independently.

A window taking up an entire wall offers

△

TOP ROW, LEFT THREE SWAGS CAN OFTEN BE USED ACROSS A DOUBLE SASH WINDOW SUCH AS THIS ONE. THE CURTAINS, PRETTY AND FLORAL, ARE OFFSET BY PLAIN PINK ON THE CORNICE, TAIL LININGS AND ROSETTES.

▷

THIS WIDE WINDOW HAS BEEN INTEGRATED INTO THE ROOM BY AN ALL-OVER TREATMENT OF TWO PATTERNS – STRIPED AND FLORAL – WITH THE CUSHIONS, LAMPSHADE AND LITTLE FOLDING SCREEN PLAYING A MINOR ROLE. THE STRIPED ROMAN SHADE IS ENCLOSED BY THE FLOWER PATTERN ON ALL FOUR SIDES.

scope for one of the more elaborate headings, as it gives room for the rhythmic effect of repeated pleats or soft smocking. The best choice would be a relatively subdued fabric – possibly even a plain, textured one. If a patterned fabric is preferred, a bold, simple design such as broad stripes can work well. When choosing the pattern and color of the curtains, you may need to take into account not only the wall treatment but also the view through the window. And the larger the area of fabric, the more important it is that it ties in well with other furnishing fabrics elsewhere in the room.

Roller shades, or Roman shades and their variations, can be used to good effect with a large expanse of glass. They are not particularly well suited to a metal-framed kind of window, but can look superb set into an elegant wooden surround.

If the window is very wide, an attractive treatment might be a large Roman shade, its flat horizontal folds bordered with a contrasting band of color. Other types of blind will tend to sag in the middle, or look blowzy and overdone, if made on such a scale. The advantage of using a series of narrow shades is that they can be kept at slightly different heights, avoiding the monotony of a continuous horizontal line at the bottom. Vertical borders on each blind will emphasize the changes of level.

If the view is unattractive, it will be necessary to screen it with some type of sheer fabric. For a large window, a subtle, neutral choice is best. Fabric with a textural quality, such as a muslin or fine voile, will pleasantly diffuse the light, create a summery mood and reduce the undesirable view to a soothing blur.

△

TOP CENTER A WINDOW ON THIS SCALE NEEDS FULL CURTAINS TO BREAK UP THE EXPANSE OF GLASS AND AVOID MONOTONY. OVERLAPPING SWAGS ON BRONZED BRACKETS RIPPLE ATTRACTIVELY ABOVE THE WINDOW, AND FALL AT THE SIDES INTO TAILS THAT ARE LINED FOR CONTRAST IN PLAIN MAROON. FRINGES IN GRAY AND MAROON FINISH OFF THE EDGES.

◁

STRIPED FABRIC MAKES A POWERFUL IMPACT IN THIS BEDROOM. THE SIMPLE CURTAINS HAVE A LARGE BOW IN THE CENTER, AND ARE FURTHER DEFINED BY CREAM BORDERS AT EACH OF THE VERTICAL EDGES.

△

A SUPERB PERIOD EFFECT. AROUND THE RIDGED POLE (NOTE THE DELICATE GARLANDS) IS ONE PIECE OF FABRIC DRAPED TO FORM FULL SWAGS WITH A MINIATURE SWAG IN THE CENTER. THE SWAGS DEVOLVE INTO TAILS ALMOST TO FLOOR LEVEL. BEHIND IS AN ELABORATE SHEER AUSTRIAN SHADE. LIKE THE MAIN FABRIC, THE SHADE HAS TWO-COLOR FRINGING.

▷

AN ENGLISH DESIGN OF 1805, FOR A STRAIGHT-SIDED BAY. THE INNER CURTAINS ARE LIKE PLAIN COLUMNS, CONTRASTING WITH THE ORNATE VALANCE, WITH ITS GRIFFINS AND MASKS, DETACHED FRINGING AND VIVID RED STRIPE.

△

THERE ARE TRICKS FOR MAKING A SMALL WINDOW LOOK LARGER. THIS ONE, IN A MANY-ANGLED ROOM, HAS BEEN CURTAINED AS IF IT WERE FULL-LENGTH TO OVERCOME THE IMPRESSION OF MEANNESS. THE FABRIC – BRODERIE ANGLAISE – HAS A DENSELY GATHERED HEADING WITH A FRILL.

△

ABOVE RIGHT THIS IS A PROBLEM SITUATION – A SMALL WINDOW IN A CORNER RECESS. THE SOLUTION OF A SIMPLE CURTAIN PATTERNED TO BLEND WITH THE WALLPAPER WORKS EXTREMELY WELL, PREVENTING A SENSE OF CRAMPED SPACE AT THE CORNER. THE CURTAIN HANGS FROM RINGS ON A POLE AND HAS A SOFT HEM THAT HAS BEEN ALLOWED TO FALL FORWARD.

▷

A SMALL WINDOW RECESSED INTO THE WALL HAS BEEN MADE TO SEEM IMPORTANT BY TAKING THE CURTAIN FAR BEYOND ITS ACTUAL CONFINES. A BRASS ROSETTE CATCHES BACK THE FABRIC.

Windows that are modest in dimensions are a perennial challenge, and one not confined to country cottages – town houses and apartments abound with them too.

The question always needs to be asked: does a small window need a curtain or shade at all? If the window is high enough in the wall, not overlooked, and not in a bedroom where light has to be excluded, the answer might be no. With woodwork painted in a color that draws attention to the window, it can become an attractive feature in its own right. You could even bestow further importance by decorating the wall around the frame – for example, with a stencilled border. This will not only increase the ornamental value of the window, but will make it seem larger.

Usually, however, some kind of dressing will be desirable – if only a simple drape of sheer or light fabric on a pole above the window.

Curtains offer an excellent opportunity to correct a proportional imbalance: for example, you could extend the track each side to create extra width. If you use a single curtain, you need to arrange it carefully, or it may look like incomplete, as if waiting for a partner to complete the pair.

A simple style will give most pleasing results. Elaborate swags and tails, however much scaled down, are not appropriate, although there are various decorative effects that you could use in reduced proportions, such as a curved valance. The heading should be not too deep. It is effective to use a pole instead of a rod, but make sure that it is of smaller diameter than usual, to keep the proportions right.

Sill-length curtains are normally preferable on small windows to full-length ones, which would tend to look unsettlingly narrow. However, if the window is ill-proportioned, it might be better to stop the curtains just below the sill to make the whole thing seem deeper.

A general rule of thumb for curtains is to opt for fabrics that are light in both weight and color, and to use plenty of material. Otherwise, the overall effect can easily look mean. Sheers are a particularly good choice, or perhaps small-patterned prints.

Shades are an obvious answer for small sash windows – perhaps plain roller shades bordered in a contrast color. Roman, Austrian and balloon shades should have their fullness reduced in proportion to their diminished size: too many billows will look cluttered.

A PAIR OF MODEST WINDOWS SET DEEP INTO REVEALS HAS CHINTZ CURTAINS FRAMING THE OPENING AND MATCHING ROLLER SHADES WITHIN. THIS APPROACH ALLOWS A GRAND TREATMENT, WITH DEEPLY RUCHED SWAGS AND RED BORDERS.

IN THIS BATHROOM, PRIVACY IS CRUCIAL. THE BOTTOM SECTION OF THE WINDOW CONSISTS OF TWO WAISTED PANELS OF MUSLIN CASE-HEADED ONTO WIRE, WITH GRAY BORDERS. THE UPPER PART IS A SIMPLE ROLLER SHADE.

TOP THIS BATHROOM WINDOW HAS BEEN COVERED WITH A TRANSLUCENT WHITE SHADE, MULTIPLIED IN AN ARRANGEMENT OF MIRRORS TO CREATE A MORE INTERESTING EFFECT.

When curtaining bays, the secret of success is to look at the window as a whole, and not as a series of separate elements. Even a bay with as many as six or seven different sections can be handled in this way, if it is well proportioned. The surround and the areas of glass must be taken equally into account. If the wooden members are narrow, it might be appropriate to use just a single pair of curtains, one at each side. However, a large window with wide, heavy-looking wooden verticals at each division would look better hung with intermediate curtains that would serve to cover the unseemly expanse of wood and correct the overall proportions.

For curtaining a bay window, rods or poles can be constructed with appropriate angles, or a curved rod may be used. (It may have to be attached to the ceiling if wall space is limited.) Special brackets with curved arms will connect straight lengths of pole. Brass poles can be bent

to order by specialist suppliers. Plastic rods are flexible, and can easily be bent to fit a curved window, provided that they are fixed securely at the stress points. Before buying a plastic rod check that it is strong enough to carry the fabric. You can buy a special metal rod to curve around a bay, but it is not easy to install, and will need more support than a straight rod.

Rectangular bays, often found in 20th-century homes, also pose a challenge. One option is to use separate lengths of lateral rod each with its own narrow side curtain, across the narrow ends of the bay. Three single shades, one for each segment, can also work well. Some people, however, might prefer a frankly theatrical curtain treatment, with overlapping sweeps of fabric – disguising the awkwardness of the corners. A valance sweeping down to voluminous tails at either side is a good way to screen off the edges of the side curtains.

▽

A SHALLOW BOW WINDOW WITH BOOK SHELVES UNDERNEATH IS DRESSED HERE WITH A BALLOON SHADE WHOSE PLEATS ARE UNDERSTATED, AND THEREFORE DO NOT INTERFERE WITH THE PRESENTATION OF THE PATTERN – A REPEATED ARCADIAN SCENE IN AN OVAL WITH GARLANDS AND EARS OF WHEAT.

△

THIS HISTORIC DESIGN FOR A THREE-BAY WINDOW IS RATHER RICHER THAN WE WOULD NORMALLY USE TODAY. THE CORNICE HOLDS A VALANCE WITH MULTIPLE SWAGS, AND TAILS AT THE CORNERS.

▽

A BROAD CORNICE SWAGGED AND TAILED, FRAMES TWO PAIRS OF CURTAINS IN A BUSY PRINT.

▷

THE GOTHIC-ARCHED CORNICE HAS SUGGESTED THE TREATMENT HERE. THE SWAGS ARE DEEP AND RICH. LINKING THE THREE SECTIONS AT THE TOP IS A ROPE WITH DECORATIVE KNOTS AND TASSELS.

▽

DRAMA IS THE KEYNOTE IN THIS BEDROOM. THE ROLLER SHADES MAKE A SUPERB CONTRAST.

△

THIS SIMPLE DRESSING WITH FRENCH PLEATS IS DESIGNED TO EMPHASIZE THE BEAUTY OF INTERSECTING ARCHES SET INTO THE DELICATE TRACERY OF A GENEROUS BAY WINDOW. THE EMPHATIC RHYTHM OF THE CURTAINS ECHOES THAT OF THE TREES OUTSIDE.

▷▷

FAR RIGHT, TOP SWAGGED AND TAILED CURTAINS IN A RICH TAN BROCADE GIVE DISTINCTION TO THIS BAY. THE TAILS, CONSISTING OF PLEATED TUBES, ONE INSIDE THE OTHER, HAVE AN ALMOST ARCHITECTURAL PRESENCE. THEY ARE EDGED WITH PLAIN FABRIC TO ECHO THE LINING. A BOW ABOVE EACH TAIL CONFERS FURTHER STATUS.

▷

THIS COMPOSITION PLACES THE EMPHASIS AT THE TOP WITHOUT RESORTING TO A VALANCE, OR TO SWAGS AND TAILS. INSTEAD, THE CURTAINS ARE LINKED BY RICH FOLDS OF CHINTZ AUSTRIAN SHADES. WHEN THE CURTAINS ARE CLOSED, THE BOLD BORDER WILL COME INTO GREATER PROMINENCE, CREATING A BOLD RHYTHM.

▷▷

FAR RIGHT, BOTTOM THIS *TOUR DE FORCE* OF A WINDOW DRESSING INCORPORATES SOLID FABRIC-COVERED ARCHES WITHIN A THEATRICAL FRAME OF CURTAINS AND SWAGS, WHICH IN TURN IS SET WITHIN BALCONIES AND TURNED COLUMNS. SHEER CAFÉ CURTAINS ADD A TOUCH OF DELICACY ABOVE FLOOR LEVEL.

SHUTTERED WINDOWS

People who live in a house with indoor shutters will have no hesitation in warmly recommending this uniquely architectural window treatment. As a barrier against cold and noise, and as a form of security (particularly when anchored by a firm iron or wooden bar), shutters have no equal.

Styles of shutters have shown an interesting development. In the 17th century, those on tall windows were often constructed in horizontal tiers so that different sections could be closed at different times to vary the amount of light and shade. By 1700 most shutters were the full height of the window. In the grander houses they had carved and molded panels designed to tie in with the decoration elsewhere in the room. In both Europe and America, painted and patterned shutters were used in fairly simple houses from the 18th century on, dispensing with the need for curtains. You can take the same approach today, allowing the shutters to shoulder all the work of ornamentation, without the distraction of fabric.

If you do decide to use fabric, positioning the curtain rail in such a way that the action of the shutters will not be obstructed requires care. The rod has to be extended from the architrave, sufficiently to allow freedom of movement, and the resulting gaps at the ends will have to be covered by an arrangement of fabric.

Shutters are not always housed in an angled reveal, but sometimes lie flush to the window frame, presenting themselves, when closed, as flat surfaces on the same plane as the wall. An effective treatment for this style of shutter would be a crown of swags and tails.

The solid 19th-century shutters still found in many town houses look particularly good when the panels are painted on both sides in colors that coordinate with accompanying curtains. At night, the curtains need not be drawn, but can be left to form a frame for the shutters. Another option is to take this idea to its extreme and frame a shuttered window with loose drapes of fabric hung over a pole.

If your curtains are patterned, choose one of the less dominant colors and use this as the main color of the shutters. Any molding can then be picked out either in white, or in a second color from the fabric.

Shades are an effective alternative with shuttered windows. Both roller and Roman shades look pleasing enclosed in the frame formed by the hinged panels. Where a window has a fixed wooden or plaster panel above it, matched to shutters which fit snugly underneath, an Austrian or Roman shade can be hung over the fixed panel to make the window seem larger.

New shutters can be made quite easily as simple hinged pairs, or alternatively you can buy them from builders' suppliers as louvered, slatted panels. If you live in a house that has lost its shutters, it is not too difficult to get replacements made.

◁

ASYMMETRICAL DRESSINGS ALLOW YOU TO SHOW OFF THE BEAUTY OF SHUTTERS BY REVEALING JUST ONE SIDE: THE EYE AUTOMATICALLY TAKES IT THAT THE OTHER SIDE IS IDENTICAL. THIS IS A CONVENTIONAL FORMAL TREATMENT, EXCEPT THAT ONE MAJOR ELEMENT IS MISSING. ON THE LEFT, THE DARK CHECK BORDERS CLEARLY SEPARATE THE SWAG AND TAIL FROM THE WOODWORK.

◁

A COMBINATION OF THE DECORATIVE AND THE PRACTICAL. THESE CURTAINS ARE CAUGHT HIGH, LIKE AN EMPIRE-LINE DRESS, TO DISPLAY THE SHUTTERS AND ALLOW THEM TO BE CLOSED WITHOUT DIFFICULTY. THE SOFT RUFFLED VALANCE RUNS THE WHOLE LENGTH OF BOTH WINDOWS, TYING THEM TOGETHER. THE ONLY OTHER ELEMENT IS A SMALL SWAG ABOVE EACH WINDOW.

△

LEAVING SHUTTER PANELS UNPAINTED HAS
CREATED AN INTERESTING DECORATIVE EFFECT IN
THIS BAY WINDOW. THE OUTER CURTAINS IN SOFT
COTTON WITH A FINE CHECK PATTERN CONTRAST
WITH INNER CURTAINS, HALF THE WIDTH, IN SHEER
FABRIC. ALTHOUGH THE POLE FROM WHICH THE
DRESSINGS HANG GOES ALL THE WAY AROUND THE
WINDOW, THE CENTRAL BAY IS LEFT UNCURTAINED:
HERE, THE SHUTTERS ALONE DO THE WORK OF
BLOCKING OUT THE LIGHT AND CREATING PRIVACY.

◁

BALLOON SHADES IN A GREEN AND BRONZE LEAF PATTERN RISING ABOVE THE TOP EDGE OF SHUTTERS DISPLAY THE DELICATE LINES OF THIS BAY WINDOW. BOTH SHADES AND SHUTTERS CAN WORK UNIMPEDED. THE WOODWORK IS DELICATELY MARBLED ALONG THE MOLDING. AT NIGHT THERE IS A CHOICE OF KEEPING THE SHADES FOLDED HIGH OR LOWERING THEM TO COVER THE WOODEN PANELS.

▽

IN THIS ELEGANT ROOM, THE WINDOWS HAVE BEEN CONCEIVED AS A WHOLE. THE WOODWORK, INCLUDING FINE SHUTTERS WITH OVAL MOLDINGS, IS PAINTED IN A RICH BLUE-GRAY, WITH CONTRASTING POLE-HUNG CURTAINS IN GRAY AND OATMEAL STRIPES, SIMPLY HUNG, WITH DOUBLE CORD TIE-BACKS. WHEN SO MUCH EMPHASIS IS PLACED ON COLOR AND SHAPE, ELABORATE DETAILS ARE NOT NEEDED.

Through half-open French doors comes the scent of new-mown grass, the sound of ball against bat, the buzzing of a lazy bee. These are sensations of quintessential summer – a reverie in which French doors play a supporting role.

When they made their first graceful appearance in 17th-century country mansions, French doors often opened onto an upper balcony By the 19th century they had moved to the ground floor, offering a route from the drawing room to the terrace. The theme was again taken up enthusiastically with the spread of suburbia.

Whether the glass doors stand alone as a pair or have additional glass at the sides (and sometimes above), the same basic treatment is appropriate: floor-length curtains that combine elegance with practicality. Outward-opening doors present no special problems, but with doors that swing inward you will often need to extend the pole or rod well beyond the sides of the frame, so that the doors can open unimpeded when the curtains are drawn back. If the doors are set into their own alcove, it is usually advisable to hang the curtains on the outside.

Side curtains can be combined with sheers behind, or with lace picture panels – antique or reproduction – attached to the door frames at top and bottom, covering the glass. Plainer lace or muslin bought by the yard or meter can also be cut to length and attached over each door by wire rods slotted through cased headings at top and bottom. If using muslin, bear in mind that it looks best when bunched and full, rather than stretched taut in a narrow strip.

The contrast of heavy outer and more lightweight inner fabric has a long tradition behind it. Historically, the heavier fabric – often with a bold design – was not always made into

◁

GLAZED DOORS SET INTO A LARGE SQUARE WINDOW-WALL OF A LIBRARY/DRAWING ROOM ARE EFFECTIVELY HIGHLIGHTED BY FRINGED, DEEP RED COTTON CURTAINS. BRONZED TIE-BACKS POSITIONED AT DIFFERENT LEVELS CREATE A LIVELY ASYMMETRICAL EFFECT AND ENSURE THAT PASSAGE THROUGH THE DOOR IS RELATIVELY EASY – EVEN IF NOT ENTIRELY UNIMPEDED.

▽

A PAIR OF TALL, NARROW GLAZED DOORS OPENING INTO A CONSERVATORY IS GIVEN THE FULL PERIOD PORTIÈRE TREATMENT, WITH SWAGS, TAILS, KNOTTED CORD AND TASSELS. THE SWAGS OCCUPY THE DEAD AREA OF WALL SPACE BETWEEN THE TOP OF THE DOORWAY AND THE BOTTOM OF THE GOTHIC CORNICE. FOR ANOTHER, MATCHING WINDOW TREATMENT ELSEWHERE IN THE SAME ROOM, SEE PAGE 67.

full curtains: sometimes it was used instead as a fairly elaborate set of drapes with a valance to show off the shape of the window and make a sharp contrast with the soft sheer curtain below. You can achieve a similar feel today by using, say, a strongly patterned chintz shaped or draped over a swathe of self-patterned or plain translucent fabric. Tie-backs on the outer curtains will allow the maximum light through and shape the drapes attractively.

Some French doors may be better served by not having curtains at all. If the window frame is elegant, a swag draped over a pole might be pleasing – and would certainly avoid the practical difficulties referred to above. A variation on this theme, first popularized in the 19th century, is to use a shawl or large scarf as a draped valance. Queen Victoria was responsible for bringing into vogue the paisley shawl, which was often seen asymmetrically draped over a French door, as if tossed carelessly over the pole, with muslin curtains below. Of course, it was not merely tossed, but was arranged with great care, and the final effect was dramatic. This idea can be borrowed today, using any interesting textiles. It is an eye-catching way to deploy a favorite oddment of fabric. If you combine two pieces of fabric, they do not even have to match.

Shades are an option for French doors, if kept relatively simple. Whereas a floor-length balloon or Austrian shade will tend to appear excessive, a plain cream roller shade can look stunning, especially inside a frame of elegant swags and tails, or even formal dress curtains. A roller shade should be attached to the door itself, or set high enough to allow free movement of the mechanism.

Glazed Doors

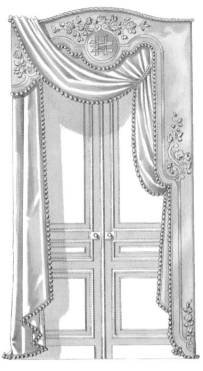

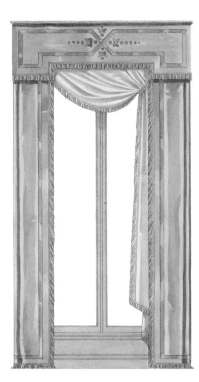

▷

In this period design for a portière, asymmetry creates drama. The door has a lambrequin—an extended cornice—falling down one side to finish at floor level, but stopping at swag level on the left. Within this frame, and closely echoing its shape, the green silk curtain is arranged to look almost casual, hung up and over the lambrequin and caught by a double cord at one corner.

▽

In a basement breakfast room, curtains patterned with flowers and exotic birds serve sliding glazed doors that lead to the patio. The curtains can be drawn to occupy the whole of the glazed wall. Their rod is hidden by a symmetrically ruffled valance fixed to a pole covered in the same fabric, with little bows creating a rhythm.

▷

French doors leading from a living room have prompted thick, flowing muslin drapes that leave plenty of room for the free flow of traffic. Above each window are swagged tails, light in weight but strong in color, falling from a medallion. There are also three white swags, the central one, more fully visible, providing a background for cords and tassels.

◁

This is a tall window rather than a doorway, but the same treatment would be adaptable to outward-opening doors. The somewhat severe cornice and straight outer curtains evoke the Renaissance. The inner curtain is caught high. The intention is to emphasize the rectangular shape of the feature rather than to subdue it with a wealth of curves.

A STONE-MULLIONED GOTHIC WINDOW IN A BATHROOM IS FLANKED BY FLORAL CURTAINS THAT DO NOT FOLLOW ITS FORM BUT ARE SWEPT BACK TO PRESENT THE WINDOW'S SHAPE AND TRACERY.

◁

A BROAD, SHALLOW ARCH CALLS FOR A THEATRICAL INTERPRETATION. THESE STEPPED FRINGED SWAGS FROM A HEADING SHAPED TO FIT THE CURVE FILL THE ROLE IDEALLY, FINISHING IN LOOSE FOLDS ON THE WINDOW SEAT. ROSETTES CREATE A SUBDUED RHYTHM ALONG THE TOP.

Windows are durable parts of the structure of a house, and therefore not too easy to change on a fashionable whim. This is why many unusually shaped windows from the past remain with us today – including stone-mullioned Gothic windows with pointed arches, and round-arched windows of a later era.

Stone mullions are typical of Elizabethan times, but they also occur in many 19th-century buildings affected by the Gothic Revival. Horace Walpole, one of the leading exponents of this movement, allowed neither shutters nor curtains to impair the lines of his Gothic windows, but not everyone agreed with this purist approach. Windows in this style were sometimes dressed, as they may be today, with fine curtains held off by high tie-backs, and with a cornice or drapery above, following (somewhat tortuously) the shape of the arch. Alternatively, a mullioned window of what might be termed average size can be curtained today in the same way as a rectangular or square window, using a straight rod or pole to hold a pair of curtains, making sure that the mullions and reveals are not hidden when the curtains are drawn back.

Windows of this type sometimes have a stone sill or ledge, deep enough and low enough to be used as a window seat – as it probably was originally. Such a ledge needs long, soft seat cushions in a fabric to complement the curtains.

More common is the round-headed window – essentially a Neo-classical form, especially popular in the 17th, 18th and early 19th centuries. A variant of this, posing a particular problem for drapers, was the Venetian-style window borrowed from the work of the 16th-century Italian architect Andrea Palladio: it took the form of a round-headed central portion, flanked by narrower rectangular side windows. Historically, the central part was often dressed with a type of festoon curtain in two parts, with obliquely set cords by which it was pulled up and apart. The side parts were covered simply with shutters. Such windows pose a problem, and when they have shutters it is probably best not to curtain them at all.

An arched curtain heading can be made to look perfectly acceptable, but it will be hard to obtain exactly the right effect every time the curtains are opened or closed. The best solution may be to keep them permanently closed at the top, and held back during the day with tie-backs, so that the gathers in the heading are not disturbed. A simpler treatment is to hang curtains from a long pole placed fairly high above the top of the arch, so that the shape of the window is fully apparent during the day.

A fine-slatted venetian blind hung over the arched window, with curtains as an outer frame, may suit some rooms. The arch will be perfectly visible through the slats during the day; at night you will have the choice of closing the shades or drawing the curtains.

Another approach, particularly suitable with Gothic-style windows, is the use of an arched valance. Rather than attempting to follow the window shape precisely, the most successful treatment is to arch the valance in a series of steps. Especially if the window has arched leading, the eye will easily visualize the arched top of the window even though its precise curves are obscured by the valance.

A ROUND-ARCHED WINDOW IS ONE OF
THE BEST POSITIONS FOR FABRIC IN
RICH FESTOONS. THIS DEEPLY
RUCHED SHADE IN A MELLOW-
COLORED DAMASK HAS A
PARTICULARLY LIVELY PROFILE. THE
DOORS OPEN INWARD, SO THIS
TREATMENT BLOCKS OFF A
THOROUGHFARE TO THE YARD
BEYOND — ITS ONE DISADVANTAGE.

◁

HEIGHT IS THE OVERRIDING
IMPRESSION IN THIS SOPHISTICATED
LIVING ROOM. THE OUTER CURTAINS
IN SELF-PATTERNED GOLDEN YELLOW
HAVE FRENCH-PLEATED HEADINGS
THAT CURVE WITH THE ARCHES OF
THE WINDOWS. THE TIE-BACKS ARE
HIGH TO LET IN PLENTY OF LIGHT
THROUGH THE STRIPED SHEERS.
DRAMATICALLY, A BRONZE FIGURE ON
A HIGH PLINTH IS SILHOUETTED
AGAINST THE CENTRAL PANEL. THE
CHAISE LONGUE COUNTERBALANCES
ALL THE VERTICALS.

◁◁

AN EFFECTIVE SOLUTION FOR A WINDOW SET INTO A SLOPING ROOF IS TO HANG THE CURTAINS CONVENTIONALLY, AND THEN HOLD THEM BACK AT THE ANGLE. HERE, PLAIN CURTAINS WITH A CASED HEADING ARE GIVEN EMPHASIS AT THE TOP BY A PURELY DECORATIVE HEAVY WOODEN POLE. BELOW, GRAVITY IS DEFEATED BY A TWISTED LENGTH OF FABRIC STRETCHED BETWEEN EXTRAVAGANT BRACKETS. THE CHEST OF DRAWERS HOLDS BACK THE LOWER LEVEL OF FABRIC.

◁

A WINDOW TOPPED BY A SKYLIGHT CAN BE VERY DIFFICULT TO CURTAIN AS A WHOLE. HERE, THE ANSWER IS TWO MATCHING SETS OF PLEATED BALLOON SHADES, THE UPPER ONES HELD INVISIBLY ON CORDS.

▽

BOTTOM LEFT ANOTHER PAIR OF DORMER CURTAINS CAUGHT WHERE THE SLOPE MEETS THE WALL, BUT THIS TIME HELD BY SIMPLE TIE-BACKS. THE PROBLEM OF THE HEADING IS SOLVED BY A THICK POLE FROM WHICH THE LACE CURTAINS HANG ON LARGE WOODEN RINGS. HEAVIER FABRICS WOULD NOT WORK IN SUCH A COMPOSITION, AS THEY WOULD PULL TOO FAR FORWARD.

Most houses possess at least one quirky, oddly positioned window slotted in to admit extra light and air. It might be simply a rectangle of glass placed inaccessibly high in a wall, or it might be a dormer, skylight or clerestory window – all of which are difficult to curtain.

Dormer windows project from an attic room (or loft conversion) with a sloped ceiling. In a room used only during the daytime, a window dressing may not be necessary. However, in a bedroom, the best answer might be traditional curtains in a lightweight fabric: if the mood is country-cottage, the effect can look extremely pretty. It is usually desirable to fix the rod or pole within the side walls, close against the window. However, if space restrictions prevent this, an interesting solution is to hang curtains on one or two hinged poles of narrow diameter,

fixed so that they can be swiveled open to rest against the dormer wall during the day. As with all small windows, the curtains should either have a small-scale pattern or be plain-colored. A sheer can be used behind, threaded onto narrow expandable poles at the top and bottom.

Skylights seldom present problems of privacy, but may require covering to diffuse some of the light, or to create a feeling of night-time seclusion and warmth. For diffusion, the obvious choice is sheer fabric anchored on thin poles at top and bottom of the sloping window. To cover the black hole of night, the most practical solution is a venetian blind (the type with a double fixing) or some sort of fabric shade– perhaps an unlined, pleated Roman shade or a roller shade–held against the window by means of a thin pole strategically placed.

Clerestory windows, an idea borrowed from ecclesiastical architecture, are positioned high in a wall to provide extra light in an area of the house that would otherwise be gloomy. They may take the form of a long pane or series of panes between the roofline proper and the top of a lean-to roof extending from a point some distance down the wall. Shades are the most suitable treatment for such inaccessible places. Their operating cord must be set far enough down the wall to be reachable.

Circular windows also tend to be in an elevated situation. They are often best left alone, especially if they include stained glass. Indeed, this may also suggest a successful treatment for a rectangular clerestory: by including stained glass you can create a striking feature whose effect would only be undermined by fabric nearby.

SMALL DORMER WINDOWS WITH CURTAINS SET AGAINST THE GLASS HAVE A COTTAGEY FEEL, ESPECIALLY IF THE FABRIC IS A PRETTY FLORAL PRINT. HERE, THE CURTAINS WORK WITH BED DRESSINGS, WALLS AND CEILING TO PRESENT A BUSY OVERALL EFFECT. THERE IS CONTRASTING RED TRIM ON THE BED VALANCES, BUT AT THE WINDOW THE PATTERN IS LEFT TO SPEAK FOR ITSELF.

THE SLOPING CEILING ABOVE THIS SMALL ATTIC WINDOW SUGGESTED AN INGENIOUS DESIGN – A TIGHTLY PENCIL-PLEATED VALANCE THAT FOLLOWS THE SLOPE, THEN FALLS AWAY TO A SOFT VALANCE. THE CURTAINS HANG SIMPLY IN FRONT OF A ROLLER SHADE, WHICH ENSURES THAT THE WINDOW IS LIGHTPROOF. USE OF FLOOR-LENGTH CURTAINS MAKES THE SMALL WINDOW APPEAR MUCH LARGER THAN IT IS.

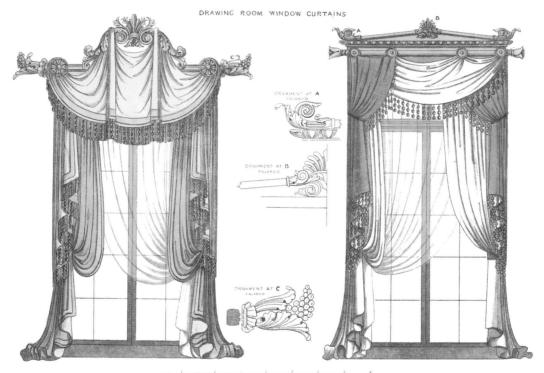

DRAWING ROOM WINDOW CURTAINS

ORNAMENT AT A
ENLARGED

ORNAMENT AT B
ENLARGED

ORNAMENT AT C
ENLARGED

SCALE · FEET

◁

CURTAINS MAKE AN IMPORTANT CONTRIBUTION TO THE STYLE OR MOOD OF A ROOM. TO FILL THIS ROLE THEY DO NOT NECESSARILY HAVE TO BE ELABORATE OR EMPHATIC. IN THIS HIGHLY INDIVIDUAL DINING ROOM, DECORATED AS AN ORIENTAL PAVILION, SIMPLE SHEERS CUT TO FIT THE ARCHES MAKE A STUNNING IMPACT. THE HEADING IS A SIMPLE ARRANGEMENT OF CORDS AND TASSELS, SILHOUETTED EFFECTIVELY AGAINST THE LIGHT-DIFFUSING FABRIC. TO DINE IN SUCH A ROOM WOULD BE PLEASURABLY RELAXING.

△

ANYONE FORTUNATE ENOUGH TO LIVE IN A GRAND PERIOD HOME, OR A MODERN HOME IN A PERIOD STYLE, HAS SCOPE FOR USING FABRIC ON A MAGNIFICENT SCALE IN A LIVING ROOM, DINING ROOM, BEDROOM OR LIBRARY. HISTORIC PRINTS MAY OFFER SOME INSPIRING IDEAS. THESE VERY COMPLEX TREATMENTS FOR A DRAWING ROOM, THE WORK OF THE DESIGNER GEORGE SMITH, WERE PUBLISHED IN 1826. TODAY'S FASHIONABLE COMPOSITIONS WITH SWAGS, TAILS AND TIE-BACKS LOOK MODEST BY COMPARISON.

LIVING ROOMS

For many people, the living room is a place – perhaps the only place – where order reigns. Calm and comfort are combined with a certain air of stateliness, appropriate for entertaining guests. For others, the need is for a family room, where everyone can relax, sit, talk and play, in an informal setting. The window treatment, more than any other single factor, sets the key. By a careful choice of curtains you can evoke an impressive grandeur or a mood of casual ease.

In many homes, the living room is the largest of rooms, with correspondingly large windows where the soft, welcoming effect of fabric can be fully exploited. It is also the room that is in most constant use, in the daytime and in the evening. Both these considerations need to be taken into account when you choose the window dressings. Often, the aim will be to let as much light in as possible during the day, and at night to make a visual impact without being excessively dominant. In order to maximize light, most people prefer the room as a whole, and the curtains in particular, to be pale-toned, but this is in fact only one option among many.

Luxurious or highly formal curtain arrangements, in expensive fabrics such as brocades or heavy silks, tend to be most successful when the rest of the room offers the same level of taste and interest. Such richness in the fabric would be incongruous with utilitarian furniture or an expanse of inferior carpet. However, you should avoid the common trap of equating grand with ornate, complex and cluttered. Luxury curtains will go perfectly well with relatively sparse furnishings and ornamentation, provided that nothing in the room, from the light fittings to the door handles, looks cheap. If your room has a cornice, frieze or ceiling medallion, so much the better, but grand curtains can work equally well in a plain box of generous size.

Many people would like a rich, traditional-style curtain arrangement in their living room, but are anxious that the effect might be overwhelming. The solution is to go for a pale monochrome or two-tone color scheme in all aspects of the room. Luxury materials such as taffetas, brocades or silks in reticent creams can look superb.

These days, a stripped, somewhat austere design is often preferred for a living room – perhaps with bare polished floorboards, neutral

BOLD-PATTERNED FLOWERED CHINTZ IN SOFT, WARM COLORS MAKES THIS ROOM LOOK WARM AND RELAXING. THE BORDERS AND TIE-BACKS ARE PLAIN RED. THE TWISTS OF THE HEADING OFFER ADDED INTEREST.

ABOVE LEFT CLASSICALLY SWAGGED AND TAILED CURTAINS IN COOL, NATURAL COLORS WORK WELL WITH THE FURNITURE. NEITHER THE PATTERN NOR THE TWO-COLOR FRINGING IS OBTRUSIVE.

SHEER CURTAINS AT THIS BAY WINDOW LET LIGHT THROUGH TO CREATE A DAPPLED WARMTH. THEY ARE CAUGHT HALF-WAY UP TO FORM DEEP SWAGS. PALE ROLLER SHADES FORM A SECOND LAYER.

upholstery and a few bright, changeable accents of color provided by ornaments, flowers or pictures. In such circumstances, soft, pale sheers, tumbling generously to the floor, can convey just the right mood.

If you like to use table and floor lamps to create distinct pools of light at night-time, heavily ruched fabrics might be a good choice: deep shadows will gather in the folds, conveying an air of mystery and sophistication. In summer, when the evenings remain light, you could pack away the heavy drapes and replace them with something more airy: seasonal changes of this kind are well worth the effort and expense.

Apart from the curtains or shades, the most prominent fabrics in the room will be those on the sofa and chairs. It is advisable to treat all these fabrics as a single composition (though not necessarily using identical colors or patterns) to tie the decoration closely together.

One simple and effective way to complement the softness of curtains, and perhaps to pick out an element in their pattern, is with vases and bowls of fresh flowers at strategic points around the room. You could even choose flowers that pick up a particular color, whether in the main fabric or in trimmings such as tie-backs or piping. If the curtains or shades are plain and simple, exotic flowers such as orchids will create a dramatic counterpoint.

△

ABOVE LEFT IN ANOTHER ROOM OF THE SAME HOUSE, A DEEPLY FOLDED SHADE IN RICH BROWN VELVET, WITH AN INTRICATE APPLIQUÉ BORDER, PRESENTS A VARIATION ON THE SAME THEME, THIS TIME OFFSETTING A FINE WINDOW WITH A BEADED WOOD SURROUND.

◁

IN AN INTERIOR THAT HAS THE SAME MELLOW, TRADITIONAL FEEL AS THE OTHER ROOMS SHOWN ON THIS PAGE, AN ANTIQUE PANEL OF TAPESTRY HAS BEEN TRANSFORMED INTO A ROLLER SHADE IMMENSE LUXURY.

◁◁

COMFORTABLE ABUNDANCE IS THE KEYNOTE OF THIS PERIOD LIVING ROOM FULL OF FINE PICTURES, STATUARY AND FURNITURE. IN THE MIDST OF SUCH PROFUSION, THE WINDOW DRESSING IS RELATIVELY SIMPLE—A DAMASK AUSTRIAN SHADE WITH THREE LAYERS OF FRINGING. THE SHADE SHOWS OFF THE PATTERN OF THE WINDOW FRAME.

LIVING ROOMS

This is the cool, calm look, appropriate with simple furniture. The wall of windows has three pairs of cream curtains falling from loose French pleats, and discreetly caught back at sill level. Behind the sofa hangs a balloon shade that leaves just enough room for a classical bust beneath.

A living room with fine period shutters at the windows and balconies outside can call for shades instead of curtains. These Roman shades have a certain formality and restraint that fit in with the overall mood. The delicate stripes on the fabric help to emphasize the windows' height.

DINING ROOMS

Some dining rooms double as additional living space, while others are devoted entirely to the arts of the table. However, quite apart from any extra functions that it has to perform, your dining room, above all, should be designed as a place in which meals become a positive pleasure.

An atmosphere of comfort is essential, and the colors of both walls and fabrics should be conducive to good digestion. Tones should usually be on the warm side, and most people prefer a soft look.

If the room is in regular daytime use, soft, delicate, light-diffusing fabrics are always attractive. However, some households reserve their dining rooms for the evening meal, and use the kitchen for breakfast and lunch. Such a timetable may encourage you to choose curtains that are deeper and richer in tone and atmosphere. In candlelight, velvets look especially impressive.

Usually, the curtains should be full enough to give a feeling of warmth and security when drawn. However, avoid over-complicated arrangements that will detract from the impact of the table setting or food.

It is always attractive to arrange some kind of visual echo linking the window treatment with the table itself – especially when the "head" of a rectangular table is neatly framed by curtains behind. It is not an especially good idea to choose tablecloths that precisely match the curtain fabric: this would usually be too obvious a contrivance. For a more subtle echo, make a color match with the napkins, the tableware, or the centerpiece if there is one. When the curtains or blinds are in primary colors, it will usually be easy to find exactly matching spring or summer flowers to make an eye-catching centerpiece.

A dining table with places laid, and chairs arranged neatly around, almost inevitably has something of a static, studied look. One way to offset this feeling would be to choose an asymmetric window dressing – for example, drapes that are waisted by a tie-back on one side only, or a valance or cornice with uneven or overlapping swags.

The brasserie look, with café curtains, perhaps in a simple blue or red check, is something that you might like to take as a starting point for imaginative modifications. However, bear in mind that if the room looks too much like a restaurant it will feel less like home.

▽

FRENCH-PLEATED CURTAINS IN BROWN AND WHITE TICKING MAKE A LOW-KEY COMPOSITION AT THE HEAD OF A DINING TABLE. THE ONLY DECORATIVE FLOURISH IS THE ADDITION OF ROSETTES IN MATCHING FABRIC ON THE TIE-BACKS. SIMPLE ARRANGEMENTS LIKE THIS ARE ESPECIALLY SUITABLE WHEN THE CURTAINS ARE CLOSE TO THE TABLE ITSELF.

▷

AGAIN, THESE STRIPED DINING-ROOM CURTAINS ARE EFFECTIVE WITHOUT PRESSING THEMSELVES TOO MUCH ON OUR ATTENTION. THE CURTAINS HANG BENEATH A NARROW CORNICE WHICH HAS BEEN COVERED WITH THE FABRIC AND GATHERED TO CREATE A RUCHED EFFECT. CATCHING BACK THE CURTAINS NEAR THE TOP, AS WELL AS AT SILL LEVEL, GIVES THEM A MORE INTERESTING SHAPE.

In many modestly sized houses and apartments, the dining room is small, with just a narrow corridor of space encircling the table. Space-saving shades would be the most practicable option in this case. Certainly, you would not want to have bunches of fabric spilling onto the floor if there is a danger of them being trampled on or caught beneath chair legs. However, you can take steps to avoid this risk by setting the table around three sides only, with the window side left empty.

The fabric in a dining room should not be of a type that gathers smells and grease. Heavy textured wools, and other fabrics that are difficult to launder or clean, should be saved for a less hazardous environment.

▷

DARK, RICH COLORS ARE APPROPRIATE IN A ROOM THAT IS USED MOSTLY IN THE EVENINGS. THE TIED-BACK OUTER CURTAINS IN SWIRLED PAISLEY COTTON HAVE AN EXOTIC FEEL, AND CONTRAST WITH AN INNER PAIR, HANGING STRAIGHT, IN KINGFISHER-BLUE CHINTZ. ALTERNATING LOOPS OF SWAGS GIVE A TURBAN-LIKE EFFECT, WITH A CROWNING CENTRAL ROSETTE IN THE BLUE.

▽

CURTAINING ON ONE SIDE ONLY SOLVES THE PROBLEM OF AN AWKWARD CORNER IN THIS DINING ROOM THAT LEADS INTO THE GARDEN VIA FRENCH DOORS. THE STRIPED CASE-HEADED CURTAIN IS PULLED BACK FAR ENOUGH TO LET IN SUFFICIENT LIGHT FOR LUNCHES OR SUMMER EVENINGS. THE PLAIN BALLOON SHADE, DEEPLY FESTOONED, IS LINED IN THE SAME MATERIAL.

A LOW-CEILING BASEMENT DINING ROOM OFTEN
HAS AN ENCLOSED, INTIMATE CHARACTER. THIS
MOOD HAS BEEN ACCENTUATED HERE BY LINING
WALLS AND CEILING IN STRIPED FABRIC, WITH
CURTAINS TO MATCH. THE ROSETTE HEARTS AND
TIE-BACK TRIMS REFLECT THE COLOR OF THE
TABLECLOTH AND THE CONTRAST FABRIC ON THE
KITCHEN SIDE OF THE DIVIDING CURTAINS.

DINING ROOMS

▷
A *TROMPE L'ŒIL* WINDOW — ONE OF A PAIR — HELPS TO MAKE THIS DINING BAY SEEM SPACIOUS AND SUMMERY. THE STRIPED CURTAINS MATCH THE CHAIRS AND TONE IN WITH WALLS AND CEILING. OVERLAPPING SWAGS SET UP A LIVELY RHYTHM.

▷▷
FULL, STRAIGHT CURTAINING ALONG THE WHOLE WALL IS OFTEN THE BEST APPROACH WHEN SPACE IS LIMITED. HERE, ABUNDANT COTTON CURTAINS IN GOLD AND BLUE, WITH A MATCHING SCALLOPED VALANCE, GOBLET-PLEATED WITH A DEEP BLUE BORDER, PROVIDE A FINE BACKDROP.

▽
A MODERN TREATMENT FOR A BASEMENT DINING ROOM WITH ONE SMALL WINDOW, A DOOR AND A RADIATOR — ALL HIDDEN AT NIGHT BY A CONTINUOUS WALL OF CURTAIN IN A RICH ABSTRACT PATTERN. THE DOMINANT BLUE IS REPEATED IN MINIATURE ON THE PENDANT LAMP AND IN THE BLUE POTTERY.

A kitchen is a place of contradictions. Most people want a kitchen that is visually appealing, but it must also be practical and easy to work in. Safety and hygiene are crucial. In a basement kitchen, it is important to let in plenty of light.

Curtains can meet the practical requirements, but usually shades are a better choice. Their clean lines mean that the window sill, working surfaces and stove are not cluttered or dangerously covered by trailing fabric.

Kitchen windows and their hangings can become extremely dirty. Cooking grease and smells are pervasive, clinging longer to fabric than to anything else. You should therefore make ease of cleaning the main criterion in your choice of window treatments. Many proofed cotton shades, or those of heavy paper, will pose problems in this respect. If you cannot afford the time to take preventative measures, it is better to choose venetian blinds, with their wipeable slats.

If you opt for curtains near a working surface, tie-backs are desirable to keep the drapes out of harm's way and to maximize light.

Kitchen windows are not normally the place for frills and furbelows – especially if the mood is high-tech. If you choose shades, the style should be clean-lined: in most situations a Roman shade will be more suitable than a ballooning Austrian shade. Curtains too should be straightforward, with a minimum of trimmings.

A pretty floral print, or plain café curtains, will go well with stripped pine. Café curtains, slid onto a pole half-way up the window, have the advantage of letting plenty of light in. In dark basements, sheers can lighten the mood – provided that they are hung out of harm's way.

◁

SILL-LENGTH CURTAINS AT A KITCHEN WINDOW ABOVE A SINK OR WORK SURFACE CAN BE DIFFICULT TO DRAW PROPERLY. HERE IS A SOLUTION USING BLUE-TRIMMED COTTON CAFÉ CURTAINS HUNG ON WHITE POLES BY SIMPLE FABRIC LOOPS – AN ARRANGEMENT THAT MAKES THEM EASY TO OPERATE.

▷

THE SHAPE OF THE LARGE ARCHED KITCHEN WINDOW HAS BEEN PRESERVED: A NARROW FABRIC-COVERED CORNICE FOLLOWS THE CURVE. CONICAL TAILS, AND BOWS THAT MATCH THE BOW MOTIFS IN THE PATTERN, ARE THE OTHER KEY FEATURES. THE SLATE COLOR IN THE PATTERN MATCHES THE WORK SURFACE.

For many people, a room set aside for reading, writing or study is one of life's greatest luxuries. Such rooms can be furnished in traditional style to create an atmosphere of mellow, studious calm. However, if you are using the room for concentrated work, a more brisk, efficient atmosphere, perhaps with shades instead of curtains, might be appropriate.

During the day, it is usually important to let in as much light as possible. Shades must pull and curtains should be fairly simple, without any low-hanging swags or drapes that might darken the room. Tie-backs can play a key role.

At night it is usually desirable to create a sealed, cocoon-like effect by means of shades or curtains that close fully and easily. If the room is for relaxed reading, choose warm colors. Burgundies have a vaguely traditional feel, but an equally successful choice might be restful green—the easiest of all colors on the eye.

In a modernistic study, equipped with the latest in Italian reading lamps, venetian blinds would have an appropriately high-tech look.

◁

TRADITIONAL COTTON PAISLEY HAS THE RIGHT FEEL FOR THIS LIBRARY, CREATING A MOOD OF COMFORT AND RELAXATION. FROM A BRASS POLE WITH FINIALS, THE CURTAINS HANG GENEROUSLY IN NATURAL FOLDS WITH A VALANCE WHOSE CURVING PROFILE IS HIGHLIGHTED BY RED FRINGING. THE FABRIC PATTERN IS REPEATED IN WALLPAPER ABOVE THE BOOKSHELVES.

△

A FORMAL LIBRARY WITH AN AIR OF ANTIQUARIAN SCHOLARSHIP HAS SIMPLE CURTAINS IN UNLINED STRIPED SILK WITH MATCHING FRINGES. HANGING ON BRASS RINGS FROM A CLASSICAL BLACK POLE WITH BRASS FINIALS, THEY SWEEP LIGHTLY TO THE SIDES OF THE WINDOW, HELD BY CORD TIE-BACKS ON DECORATIVE DISKS. SHEER DRAPES BEHIND FILTER THE LIGHT.

△

THE ATMOSPHERE HERE IS ONE OF CONCENTRATED WORK RATHER THAN GENTEEL BROWSING. TO PROVIDE PROTECTION FROM THE GLARE OF THE SUN, THE FABRIC SHADE HAS BEEN LOWERED TO THE BOTTOM HALF OF THE WINDOW. HOWEVER, WHEN THE DESK IS NOT IN USE THE TOP OF THE SHADE CAN BE WINCHED TO THE HEAD OF THE WINDOW, LETTING MORE LIGHT IN.

Many halls are without windows, and thus have no need of conventional curtains. However, in a long and narrow hall a portière (that is to say, a curtain hung over the doorway) can serve a useful purpose. At the entrance door it can cut out drafts; at the opposite end of the hall it can be used to mark a definite barrier between the entrance-way and the house proper.

If there happens to be a window on one of the walls of the hallway, a discreet curtain treatment might be called for – perhaps using the minimum of fabric to let in the maximum of light.

Many staircases have windows that need no curtaining at all: the best approach may be to keep them entirely unveiled to eliminate dangerous dark corners.

Stairwell windows are more difficult to deal with than windows on a half-landing, because the structure of the staircase itself often means that they are not in proportion to other windows in the immediate vicinity. If other window dressings are in view, it is important to draw the stairwell windows into the same general composition. You could use either the same fabric or a modified version of the same design. Shades may be better than curtains: keep them light in color and weight.

A half-landing window is likely to be one of the most interesting architectural features of the house. Often it will have a distinctive shape. It may be preferable to leave such a window uncurtained – especially if the half-landing is not overlooked by neighbors and there is no particular need to provide insulation.

▷

CURTAINING CAN BE USED IN HALLS AND ON LANDINGS TO MARK SPATIAL BOUNDARIES AND SOFTEN HARD-EDGED ANGLES. IN THIS HALL, A DECORATIVE DRAPE MAKES THE FINE STAIRCASE EVEN MORE DISTINCTIVE. IT IS NOT INTENDED TO BE DRAWN, AND CAN THEREFORE HANG PERMANENTLY ON FIVE HOOKS AT CORNICE LEVEL.

▷▷

SOME HALLS, IF THEY ARE WIDE ENOUGH, CAN BE TREATED RATHER LIKE LIVING ROOMS, WITH LUXURIOUS TOUCHES THAT CREATE AN AMBIENCE OF COMFORT. THIS ROOM, WITH FRENCH DOORS LEADING TO THE GARDEN, IS PRIMARILY A CIRCULATION ROUTE. HOWEVER, ITS FUNCTION IS DISGUISED BY THE FURNITURE AND BY PATTERNED VELVET DRAPES WITH SWAGS AND TAILS, AND SUMPTUOUS BALLOON SHADES BEHIND.

△

A LANDING AT THE TOP OF STAIRS IS A PLACE WITH
WHICH WE HAVE DAILY CONTACT: IT IS THUS A
SUITABLE POSITION FOR AN INTERESTING WINDOW
DRESSING — IN THIS CASE, FULL-LENGTH RICH
PAISLEY CURTAINS WITH MATCHING SWAG,
ROSETTES AND TAILS, WITH A TWO-COLOR FRINGE
AND CHAIN TIE-BACKS. THE FRIEZE HAS A
DIFFERENT, BUT HARMONIZING, PATTERN.

△

VOILE CURTAINS ON THIS LANDING FALL FROM A
DECORATIVE WOODEN POLE, ARE PARTED BY THE
GLASS-FRONTED CABINET AND SWEEP OUT TO
ROPE TIES AT THE FARTHEST EDGES OF THE SPACE.
THIS TREATMENT NOT ONLY LETS PLENTY OF LIGHT
IN, BUT ALSO CREATES AN EFFECT OF HARMONIOUS
BALANCE IN AN AREA OF THE HOUSE THAT MIGHT
OTHERWISE SEEM PURELY FUNCTIONAL.

A MEZZANINE LANDING IS TREATED AS A FORMAL DISPLAY AREA, WITH PICTURES, FURNITURE AND FIGURES CLUSTERED AROUND NARROW CURTAINS TOPPED WITH SWAGS AND TAILS AND A PATTERNED AUSTRIAN SHADE. THE SWAGS SWEEP UP TO AN APEX, THEIR ANCHOR POINTS HIGHLIGHTED BY MALTESE CROSSES. THE CURTAINS ARE PLAIN, BUT ALL OTHER ELEMENTS DARKLY FRINGED.

A SHUTTERED HALL WINDOW HAS BEEN DRESSED WITH A PLEATED ROMAN SHADE TO MAXIMIZE THE USE OF SPACE: CURTAINS IN THIS AWKWARD AREA MIGHT SEEM TOO CRAMPED. THE HEADING OF THE SHADE IS HIDDEN BY AN ARCHITECTURAL CORNICE. THERE IS A FRINGE AT THE BOTTOM EDGE AND A CORD TRIM ACROSS THE WIDTH OF THE SHADE (JUST BELOW CORNICE LEVEL IN THIS PICTURE).

Privacy is a precious commodity, which we expect to find in the bedroom if nowhere else in the home. Ideally, a bedroom is a haven, a place of retreat. Furnishings and curtains must work together to ensure that a suitably restful atmosphere is created.

In a bedroom, perhaps more than in any other room, you need to be able to control the amount of light that enters – or to shut out light altogether if you wish. Choose your curtains with this in mind. If you want a feeling of comforting enclosure and you are using curtains alone, they should always be lined. If the windows face the rising sun, it might be sensible to use a special light-excluding fabric.

When used with shades, curtains can have a lighter feel. The simplest accompaniment is roller shades, but some might find this choice too hard-edged. If you want a softer mood, Roman shades look smarter than Austrian shades and work better with long, flowing curtains.

Sheer fabrics, perhaps combined with heavier outer fabrics, are always interesting in a bedroom. Muslins, laces (both patterned and plain) and other sheers that gleam in dim light all help to set up a mood of airiness and charm.

The most popular patterns for a bedroom are those that are light and bright. People tend instinctively to avoid the more sombre, heavier fabrics that might be suitable elsewhere in the house. However, you can also view the bedroom as a place for unconventional treatments: your time spent here awake is limited to a few hours a day at most, so you can afford to select designs that would be too emphatic for more prolonged exposure. For opulence, you could choose richly colored silk taffeta, luxurious brocades or swagged chintz.

Dressing the bed is one of the most enjoyable tasks of interior decoration. Even the simplest of beds can be made to look extremely pretty with fabrics. A bed in an alcove, or against a wall, or set in a simple framework of posts (or even telescopic metal poles, of the kind used in photo studios), can be dressed as simply or as elaborately as you wish. Nothing could be easier than hanging, from the center point above a bed, yards of white muslin or cheesecloth, loosely caught like a mosquito net. At the opposite end of the scale you could bedeck a half-canopy or four-poster in full curtains with swags and tails. Some further design possibilities are offered on pages 152-9 of this book.

There should be a definite relationship between the bed and the window dressing, although there is no need to be too literal-minded about this. The echo might be just a matter of details—say, bed cushions reiterating the color of curtain trimmings, or fringes of tasseled braid linking the fabric elements that harmonize but are not identical. The crown of a bed might be

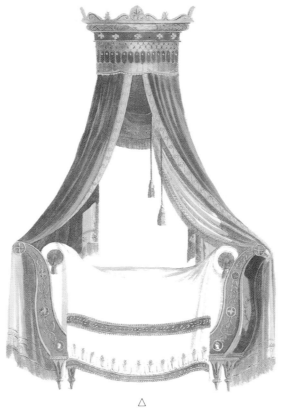

△

FRENCH BED DESIGNS WERE VERY FASHIONABLE IN THE EARLY 19TH CENTURY. THIS ELABORATE COMPOSITION FOR AN EMPIRE DAY BED WAS PUBLISHED IN 1817. FROM A GILDED CENTRAL CROWN, GREEN VELVET CURTAINS FALL, BORDERED WITH GOLD.

◁

THIS BEDROOM IS UNIFIED BY A FERN-PATTERN FABRIC. THE CROWN ABOVE THE BED HAS DEEP SWAGS WHICH ECHO THE VALANCE OVER THE WINDOW. A DELICATE PALE GREEN PATTERN PROVIDES CONTRASTING CALM ABOVE THE BED HEAD AND OVER THE BEDSIDE TABLE.

△△

NICE TOUCHES IN A ROOM OF HEIGHT-EMPHASIZING STRIPES ARE THE MIRROR ABOVE THE BED-HEAD, AND THE CURTAIN WITH ITS PLAIN TAIL AND SWAG, ONE ON TOP OF THE OTHER, OVER A STRIPED CORNICE.

△

THIS DESIGN IS BASED ON TWO HARMONIZING PATTERNS USED AT EVERY OPPORTUNITY — IN THE FABRICS AND ON THE WALLPAPER. THE ONLY STRIKING CONTRAST COMES FROM GREEN CUSHIONS.

△△

SILVERY COOLNESS IS THE DOMINANT NOTE HERE — IT IS ALMOST LIKE A FAIRYTALE ICE PALACE. THE RELATIVELY SIMPLE WINDOW AND BED DRESSINGS OWE EVERYTHING TO SUMPTUOUS FABRICS.

△

FOUR DRAPES SLUNG FROM A CORONET SWEEP TO ALL CORNERS OF A BED. THEY ARE ANCHORED TO POSTS WHICH THEMSELVES ARE SHEATHED IN FABRIC. THE RIBBON MOTIF IS ECHOED BY REAL RIBBONS.

closely tied in to the valances rather than to the curtains themselves. One word of warning: do not make the bed arrangement overdressed in relation to the windows, or it will swallow up everything else in the room.

Children's bedrooms require special care: too often the child is thought of more as a cliché than as an individual. Not all children want their window dressings and walls awash with aeroplanes, rabbits and the like, and not all girls love pink. Regardless of the wall treatment, the best choice for the window is often a simple shade, perhaps in a bold, bright color, or with timeless motifs such as geometric shapes.

▽

GREEN BOBBLED FABRIC USED AS A LINING FOR THIS CORONETED BED DRESSING IS ECHOED IN TEXTURE, THOUGH NOT IN COLOR, BY THE RED FRILLS ON THE DRAPES AND CUSHIONS. THE BEDSIDE TABLES ARE COVERED VERY SIMPLY IN THE MAIN PATTERNED FABRIC.

◁

A BEDROOM ENTIRELY COVERED IN DEEPLY PLEATED CREAM FABRIC WITH A WAVY VALANCE AS A FRIEZE HAS A TENT-LIKE AMBIENCE. THIS IS THE IDEA OF A BED CANOPY TAKEN TO ITS DRAMATIC EXTREME. THE WALL COVERING IS IN SERIES OF PANELS MEETING AT THE DADO. THE BED, BY CONTRAST, IS TREATED WITH PURIST SIMPLICITY AND THE FURNITURE IS KEPT TO A MINIMUM.

BEDROOMS AND BEDS

△

PINK AND GRAY IS A CLASSIC BEDROOM
PARTNERSHIP, TEAMED HERE TO ELEGANT EFFECT.
THE BED HAS A SHALLOW CANOPY WITH DEEP-
PLEATED SWAGS, DOUBLE TAILS AND BOWS AT
CEILING LEVEL, THE SWAGS CONTINUING AROUND
THE SIDES. THE CURTAINS SEPARATE THE TWO
COLORS—PINK ON ONE SIDE, GRAY ON THE
OTHER. ABOVE THEM IS A SIMPLE DRAPE SWAGGED
AND TAILED OVER A POLE.

▷

A STATELY BEDROOM WITH HALF-CANOPY BED HAS
A FEMININE MOOD—THANKS TO HEAVY FESTOONS
OF CREAMY YELLOW SILK, AN ABUNDANCE OF BOWS
AND ROSETTES, PATTERNED SHEERS USED BOTH
AT THE WINDOW AND AS A LINING ABOVE THE
HEAD-BOARD, AND A PILE OF FLOUNCY CUSHIONS,
LIGHT AS GOSSAMER. THE VALANCES OF THE BED
AND THE WINDOW ARE AN EXACT MATCH. IN SUCH A
ROOM THE CHANDELIER LOOKS ALMOST
UNDERSTATED.

◁◁

THE FOUR-POSTER IS STILL MUCH ADMIRED AND OFFERS A WEALTH OF POSSIBILITIES. HERE THE PRETTY BLUE FLORAL BED DRESSING IS ECHOED IN A SOFA. THIS GIVES ADDED EMPHASIS TO THE FOOT OF THE BED, MAKING THE COMPOSITION AS A WHOLE, FRAMED BY A VALANCE AT THE TOP AND THE MATCHING SKIRT OF THE SOFA AT THE BOTTOM, SEEM MORE INTERESTING AND COMPLEX. READING LAMPS MOUNTED INSIDE THE CANOPY ARE A NOVEL VARIATION ON THE THEME.

◁

THIS IS A RELATIVELY SIMPLE APPROACH TO A FOUR-POSTER IN DARK-STAINED WOOD. THE PATTERN OF PINK FLOWERS IS JUXTAPOSED WITH SOLID AREAS OF PINK IN THE LINING AND SIDE PANELS. PLAIN WHITE ROSETTES AT THE OUTSIDE CORNERS PROVIDE THE ONLY DETAIL.

◁◁

FAR LEFT, BELOW THE SHEER EXUBERANCE OF THIS EXOTIC BEDROOM, VIBRANT WITH PATTERN, WOULD BE ASTONISHING AT THE FIRST ENCOUNTER. THE BED POSTS ARE MANTLED IN FABRIC DRESSED TO MAKE WAISTED PILLARS. A PAVILION-STYLE ROOF WITH ORNAMENTAL BALLS, AND A SPECKLED RED LINING UNDERNEATH (MATCHED TO THE ROMAN SHADES AT THE WINDOW), CROWNS THE AFFAIR. LITTLE SKIRTS ON THE BEDSIDE TABLES CARRY THROUGH THE SAME THEME. AMIDST ALL THIS PATTERN, THE JAPANESE PRINT SEEMS TO FLOAT ODDLY IN SPACE.

◁

A WHITE FOUR-POSTER DRESSED ENTIRELY IN WHITE, WITH A BLUE TRIM TO ARTICULATE THE DESIGN AND A BLUE AND WHITE PATTERNED LINING INSIDE THE DRAPES. AROUND THE TOP IS A NARROWLY PLEATED CORNICE COVERED ABOVE THE DRAPES BY RUFFLED VALANCES. A LARGE ROSETTE BENEATH THE CANOPY FORMS A CENTRAL POINT TO WHICH LINES OF BLUE BRAID LEAD THE EYE. THE CURTAINS, WITH SWAGS AND TAILS AND THE SAME BLUE TRIM, PRESENT A HARMONIZING EFFECT.

▷

THE CHOICE OF GLAZED COTTON FABRIC AND SUMPTUOUS COLORS MAKE THIS BED DRESSING LOOK RICH, BUT THE DESIGN IS SIMPLE. ALL FOUR POSTS ARE CURTAINED. THIS TYPE OF DRESSING COULD EASILY BE MADE FUNCTIONAL RATHER THAN MERELY DECORATIVE: THAT IS, THE CURTAINS COULD BE CLOSED AT NIGHT. THE LINING IS STRIPED — ECHOING THE STRIPED BROWN AND WHITE BORDER ALONG THE TOP AND BOTTOM OF THE VALANCE AND ON THE EDGES OF THE DRAPES.

BEDROOMS AND BEDS

△

THE BUTTERFLY PRINT IN WHICH THIS
DIVAN IS DRESSED IS REPEATED ON
WALLS AND CEILING – REMOVING THE
VERTICAL EMPHASIS, THIS MAKES THE
ROOM SEEM LARGER.

▽▽

ANOTHER ALL-OVER TREATMENT.
RED AND GREEN FLORAL BORDERS
LINK THE RIBBON PATTERN OF THE
BED DRESSING AND WALLS WITH THE
FLORAL BALLOON SHADE.

A CANOPY HIGHLIGHTS THIS BED IN ITS OWN ALCOVE. THE DRAPE, SLUNG ON A SPEAR-ENDED POLE, IS BORDERED IN GRAY CHECK SET DIAGONALLY, WITH GREY TASSELS ALONG THE POLE. THE WINDOW CURTAINS ON A CURVED TRACK HAVE TIE-BACKS IN THE SAME CHECK AND FABRIC-COVERED BUTTONS ALONG THE GOBLET PLEATS.

A STRIKING ASPECT OF THIS BEDROOM IN PURIST WHITE IS THE RECTANGULAR CORONET OVER THE BED, ORNAMENTED WITH BOWS. THE TEMPTATION TO INTRODUCE VIVID COLOR ACCENTS IN TRIMMINGS AND CUSHIONS HAS BEEN RESISTED.

TOP TWIN BEDS ARE UNITED INTO A SINGLE, HIGHLY SYMMETRICAL COMPOSITION BY NARROW WALL-MOUNTED CORONETS IN SOFT WHITE MUSLIN AND A SKIRTED DRESSING TABLE.

BATHROOMS

Far from being just a utility room, the bathroom has become a status symbol – a place for conscious design. While still primarily functional, it has exchanged an image of frosty efficiency for one of style and luxury.

Window treatments are just as important as the provision of an attractive yet serviceable floor covering. Even if the window is filled with opaque glass, some sort of dressing may be desirable – not only to keep out drafts but also to provide some kind of antidote to the hard, shiny surfaces in which bathrooms abound.

Many fabrics do not respond well to a jungle-like atmosphere of the average bathroom. Damp, steam and extremes of temperature can damage fabrics, or even rot them. Heavy wools, for example, will retain moisture, and delicate fine silks can easily tear when wet. The best fabric for curtains or shades is undoubtedly

cotton, in its many manifestations (though unwashable glazed chintzes should probably be kept for another room).

Many of the wide range of sheer curtains now available would look good in the bathroom, perhaps combined with outer curtains if privacy after dark is needed. Another option would be a lace curtain to give privacy during the day, and shutters for seclusion and insulation at night.

To withstand condensation and heat, venetian blinds, wood and cane blinds or slatted shutters would be an excellent choice for those whose heart is not set on fabric. However, if you do choose curtains, remember that if they are bunched tightly together on the rod they will be slow to dry out. Carpets or floors can easily get wet too, so avoid letting curtains drag on the floor. Café curtains might be a worthwhile choice for a window that opens at the top.

△△
AUSTRIAN SHADES IN A FINE BLUE CHECK GO WELL WITH A BLUE AND WHITE FIGURATIVE WALLPAPER IN THIS SMALL BATHROOM WITH A PEDESTAL BASIN. THE MIRROR SURROUND IS COVERED IN THE SAME FABRIC AS THE SHADE – A SMALL DETAIL, BUT ONE THAT MAKES ALL THE DIFFERENCE. PIECES OF BLUE AND WHITE POTTERY HERE AND THERE PICK UP THE SAME COLOR THEME.

◁
A CURTAINED BATH ALWAYS HAS A LUXURIOUS AIR. HERE THE EFFECT OF A BLUE STRIPED CURTAIN CASE-HEADED ONTO A WOODEN POLE WITH FINIALS IS MADE GRANDER STILL BY THE REFLECTION IN A LARGE EXPANSE OF MIRROR. OF COURSE, FABRICS SO CLOSE TO THE BATH NEED TO BE CHOSEN WITH AN EYE TO PRACTICALITIES: THEY ARE BOUND TO GET A REGULAR SOAKING.

▷
A SIMPLE WHITE POLE SUPPORTS THIS PAIR OF CURTAINS OVER A BATH SET INTO ITS OWN ALCOVE. THE BLUE AND WHITE FABRIC AND WALLPAPER HAVE AN APPROPRIATE PATTERN OF SWAGS, WHICH ON THE AUSTRIAN SHADE COME TO LIFE IN THREE DIMENSIONS. BLUE RIBBONS LINKING THE PICTURES, AND A LITTLE BLUE CHAMBER POT, COMPLETE THE COMPOSITION.

▷
A SUPERBLY SIMPLE TREATMENT – BALANCED GRECIAN SWAGS CLEVERLY DESIGNED NOT ONLY TO PLEASE THE EYE BUT ALSO TO KEEP THE FABRIC WELL AWAY FROM THE BATH. FROSTED GLASS SOLVES THE PRIVACY PROBLEM. THE FABRIC COLOR IS TONED TO PICK UP THE FLECKS IN THE BATH SURROUND. THE MIRROR AND WALL LAMPS REINFORCE THE SYMMETRICAL EFFECT.

BATHROOMS

▽

THESE BATHROOM DRAPES ARE
DRAMATICALLY DIFFERENT — THEY
CONSIST OF A SINGLE LENGTH OF
MATERIAL WRAPPED ARTFULLY
AROUND A POLE. VENETIAN BLINDS
PROVIDE FLEXIBLE LIGHT CONTROL.

▷

ROMAN SHADES OFFER A SOLUTION
THAT IS PRACTICAL AND SMART, IN A
PSEUDO-ROMAN BATHROOM WITH A
CLASSICAL BUST. THE BROAD
STRIPES TONE WITH THE MARBLED
WALLS AND CORNICE.

△

SIMPLE AND AIRY, THESE LONG SPOTTED VOILE
CURTAINS AND ROLLER SHADE MATCHED TO THE
WALLPAPER PATTERN CAN BE CLOSED
INDIVIDUALLY OR TOGETHER, OFFERING DIFFERENT
LEVELS OF LIGHT DIFFUSION. THE CORNICE HAS A
GENTLY CURVED HEADING AND FRILLED BORDER AT
THE BASE. THE RED TRIM AT THE BOTTOM OF THE
SHADE IS JUST WIDE ENOUGH TO DELINEATE ITS
SCALLOPED EDGE.

▷

A PAIR OF ORNATE DRESS CURTAINS WITH SWAGS
AND TAILS PROVIDES LUXURY IN THIS STATELY
BATHROOM EQUIPPED WITH A GRAND CHANDELIER.
BETWEEN THE TWO LAYERS, SHEER DRAPES,
DELICATELY PATTERNED, OFFER PRIVACY IN THE
DAYTIME, WHILE AT NIGHT THE INNER CURTAINS
CAN BE CLOSED BY A HIDDEN CORD WITHOUT
UNLOOSING THE TIED-BACK OUTER PAIR.

△

AUSTRIAN OR BALLOON SHADES ARE A WAY TO MAKE GOOD USE OF DEEPLY FOLDED FABRIC WITHOUT CLUTTERING WORK SURFACES BENEATH THE WINDOW. IN THIS EXAMPLE, UNLINED BALLOON SHADES ABOVE THE WASHBASIN ARE SET AT JUST THE RIGHT LEVEL TO ALLOW LIGHT WHERE IT IS NEEDED WITHOUT COMPROMISING PRIVACY. THEIR PATTERN BRINGS TO LIFE A ROOM THAT IS OTHERWISE RATHER PLAIN, WITH AUSTERELY STRIPED WALLS.

◁

THIS AUSTRIAN SHADE, WITH A FRILLED BORDER ON ALL FOUR SIDES, IS IN A LOVELY CHINTZ WHOSE WARMTH AND RICHNESS ARE ENHANCED BY THE PROXIMITY OF A DOWNLIGHTER SET INTO THE CEILING. THE ROOM IS ON AN UPPER FLOOR OF THE HOUSE AND IS NOT OVERLOOKED, SO THE SHADE CAN BE LEFT FAIRLY HIGH IN THE DAYTIME.

THE ESSENTIALS

△

ELABORATE CURTAIN TREATMENTS SUCH AS THIS CAN LOOK FORBIDDINGLY COMPLICATED TO THE UNINITIATED. EVEN A MORE STRAIGHTFORWARD MODERN ARRANGEMENT MIGHT SEEM DIFFICULT TO PLAN IN ADVANCE. THE BEST APPROACH IS TO BUILD UP A COMPOSITION SLOWLY AND CAREFULLY, STEP BY STEP, MAKING SURE THAT EVERY ELEMENT EARNS ITS PLACE. FOR UP-TO-DATE INFORMATION ON THE HARDWARE AVAILABLE, BROWSE IN SPECIALIST STORES AND TALK TO THE EXPERTS.

▷

CURTAINS AND SHADES, COMBINED HERE TO MAKE A PLEASING CONTRAST, EACH FOLLOW THEIR OWN CONSTRUCTION PRINCIPLES, ACCORDING TO THE PARTICULAR STYLE YOU CHOOSE. ONCE YOU HAVE SELECTED THE BASICS — MATERIALS, SHAPE AND HEADING — YOU CAN TURN TO THE DETAILS. HERE, A DISTINCTIVE ARROW-SHAPED POLE, A BRASS ROSETTE BRACKET FOR THE TASSELED TIE-BACK AND A KNOTTED CORD IN THE TOP CORNER OF THE SHADE FOR BALANCE, MAKE ALL THE DIFFERENCE.

When selecting a style for curtains or shades, it is the room's architecture, and in particular the style and proportion of the windows and their surrounds, that provides the restraining element in a choice that would otherwise be almost limitless. This is, after all, the existing framework, and is unalterable – unless you are amenable to major restructuring. Provided that the structure you have is sound and generally comfortable to live with, it is best to use it as the starting point for the window treatment.

As a general rule, where you have a wood architrave framing the window, as opposed to a plaster recess, it is visually more "correct" to keep curtain arrangements within this given architectural width rather than to extend beyond it – that is, unless there is something wrong with the proportions of the window which curtains hung outside the frame can help to disguise. (It is, of course, easier to fix into wood than into plaster.)

If the window is set back within a plaster recess, it is more logical to place the curtain fixings *outside* the recess. This arrangement admits maximum light, and does not encumber the window with too much fabric. In such cases, a single curtain may be preferable to paired curtains. This is certainly the most effective treatment for French doors – for practical as well as aesthetic reasons, as it maximizes light and leaves the operational door curtain-free.

Where to stop a curtain, in terms of length, is a decision that leaves many people completely puzzled. What if there is a radiator beneath? If the window is relatively shallow, with a sill, and with plenty of wall round it, how far should the curtains fall beneath the sill?

Again, there is a general rule that will help in such situations: the curtains should be floor length, unless the window is particularly small (in which case, see the guidelines on pages 64–5). If you can feasibly remove a radiator from beneath a window, then do so: otherwise, keep the area of coverage to a minimum to avoid losing heat. Floor-length curtains are best even with a radiator, but keep them tied back with tie-backs when not drawn. Do not interline curtains which will fall in front of a radiator, or you will keep heat out of the room in the evening.

The shape of a curtain or drape will be determined by the treatment of its heading. One option is narrow, closely arranged pleats, which you can achieve by use of curtain tapes. Varying depths of tape will produce different styles of heading and affect the "line" of the curtain, and whether it will hang formally or informally. Hand-sewn headings are not worth the effort if you also have the option of purpose-bought tapes. However, they do come into their own with French (or pinch) pleats, and goblet or smocked headings, where tapes will simply not do! With these styles (suitable for elegant formal rooms), hand-sewn headings allow the curtain to

▽

AN ORNATE ARRANGEMENT SUCH AS THIS MIGHT BE SUITABLE FOR A FORMAL ROOM IN PERIOD STYLE. THE CURTAINS HANG BELOW A MAJESTIC FLEMISH HEADING WITH SWAGGED VALANCE.

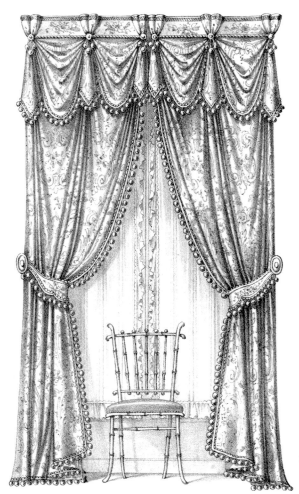

fall in well-defined deep pleats, which will need to be "dressed in" (see below) when the curtain is hung. Plainer fabrics show off the pleating to best effect.

An invaluable aid to the way that a curtain drapes or falls, or frames a window, is the humble tie-back. Tie-backs can be simply a means by which the curtain is "taken-off" the window when drawn back, maximizing light and preventing the weight of the curtain from pulling down on the rod or pole. However, for a tie-back that will truly "hug" the curtain, becoming an integral part of the whole effect rather than a superfluous band, you should opt for rope cords, in cotton or silk – or plaited fabric ties, which are the poor man's version, although equally effective.

The curtain heading, whether plain rod-pocket (cased), tape-gathered or elaborately hand-pleated, will only go so far in shaping your design ideas – ultimately it is the fabric that will convey the desired effect. The influence of architectural style over fabric choice is very strong, but should not be binding. For example, in a period interior elaborately arched windows and deep recesses will look superb decorated with full curtains in brocades or damask with swags and tails; however, a plain shade in fine Indian cotton could be just as effective, depending on the overall scheme of the room.

Most styles of curtains can be made successfully with any fabric. The choice of fabric, combined with the fixture style, will do more than anything else to determine the overall effect. The simplest is a rod-pocket curtain. Made in a richly-woven striped fabric to hang floor length from a heavy brass curtain pole, this would not look out of place, for example, in a dark-toned formal dining room. Imagine the same curtain but in natural raw silk, or unbleached muslin, caught back with a contrasting dark-colored rope tie – a different effect, lighter, yet still classical. In the same room, a more dramatic impression could be achieved if the pole were gray steel with brass spear-ends, and the curtains, bunching a little on the floor, made in a traditional *toile de Jouys* print.

Fabric is tremendously versatile. For a dramatic effect at a large single window, inexpensive sheer fabric can look wonderful draped over a pole in numerous little folds that fall in one cascade to the floor. The same fabric, used as a pair of sheer curtains behind a heavier, richer main fabric, can achieve the softness required to diffuse light from the window, at the same time creating a textural contrast with the main curtain fabric.

A combination of fabrics, with contrasting patterns, colors or textures, used within an arrangement of curtains, can enrich the whole effect. Contrasting colors may look wild and dramatic or – as with blue and white – stark yet classical.

If several fabrics are being used at the same window, in a layered series (for example, roller shades, muslin curtains and full floor-length curtains), you have to consider the effects that each will have against the others. Juxtaposition of color, pattern and texture can work very successfully but does need careful thought. When several elements are hung together at one window, the fitting details become more complex.

To make the curtains look full and luxurious use interlining – a soft blanket layer between fabric and lining which will also improve insulation. For a finishing touch, include a border, in a contrasting fabric, running vertically, set in from the edge of the curtains. The border fabric can be of different color or texture from the main fabric – perhaps a length of old, delicately patterned silk or paisley cotton. Borders always help to define the shape of a curtain or blind, and help to make a striking visual impact.

Once you have decided on the style of your curtains, they must be carefully hung and "dressed in". This term, in common usage among interior designers, refers simply to the arranging of curtains in pleats or folds, after hanging. French-pleat curtains should have even pleats all the way down from heading to floor. Other curtain headings also depend on being arranged neatly. It is also worth steaming curtains after they are hung – or, at least, pressing them well beforehand. Such attention to detail really improves the look of the composition.

▷

GOBLET-PLEATED CURTAINS, UNDERSTATED IN NEUTRAL FABRICS, HANG FROM A CURVED ROD. THE CONTRAST BORDER ALONG THE LEADING AND LOWER EDGES, AND PICKED OUT IN LITTLE BUTTONS AT THE BASE OF THE PLEATS AND IN THE TIE-BACKS, DEFINES THE OVERALL SHAPE.

A window is usually the focal point of an interior, drawing maximum attention to itself. It is thus essential when planning your window arrangement that it complements the decorative style and, no less importantly, the proportions of the room.

It is also crucial to pay close attention to detail. A mistake – for example, an out-of-proportion rosette, uneven lengths of tail, or a carelessly finished hem or fringing – will be all too obvious. This is especially true if the arrangement is a formal one. However, even relatively casual compositions need to be planned and executed with care: an informal style should not be used as an excuse for slapdash workmanship. To the visitor, viewing the window dressing for the first time, the essential impact should be exactly as you intended it – a perfect match between conception and execution.

With any curtaining, you need to decide on the degree of fullness required. As a rule of thumb you should allow two to two and half times the finished width. Remember to add overlaps and returns if you are fitting the curtains to a track. Drapes, wound around a pole, need about the same fullness allowance. Loose drapes with a single swag across the window will require only one-and-a-half times fullness.

Proportion is vitally important. Classically, a window is half as wide as it is high. As far as possible, use the window as a template for the proportions. Sometimes, however, you will want the fabric to be proportioned differently to disguise an awkward shape. If the window seems too wide for its height, fix the rod or pole higher than it would be normally. Usually, poles, rods or valances are fitted with their top level with the window architrave. If this is not possible – for example, if you are extending over the frame edge – the brackets will have to be fixed into the plaster. Extending the rod or pole beyond the sides of the frame is essential when you want to maximize the amount of light entering the room. However, with very wide windows this is not normally such a crucial consideration.

Accurate measuring is an essential ingredient of success in any window dressing or bed arrangement. If you are doing the work yourself, you must first make sure that you are properly equipped. You will need a steel ruler to measure the window dimensions. Measure *both* vertical sides for curtain drops: in old houses especially, subsidence has often caused the windows to become slightly distorted. A good way around the problem is to have fabric bunching on the floor, which means that you do not have to make each curtain to a separate measurement. Sometimes you will need to use a level (especially with shades) to check accuracy. Precision of measurement is particularly important with a recess fitting – that is, a shade or curtain fitted within a window reveal.

△

THE ASYMMETRICAL ARRANGEMENT THAT TRANSFORMS THIS ORDINARY WINDOW DEPENDS ON PRECISION. THE TWO CURTAINS, EACH HUNG ON A SEPARATE POLE, BLEND TOGETHER EFFORTLESSLY, THE CLEVERLY ANGLED CORD THAT HOLDS AND SHAPES THE HEAVIER CURTAIN CONTINUING THE CURVE OF THE LIGHTER ONE, DEFINED BY AN EXQUISITE FRINGE. THE GENEROUS FULLNESS IN EACH CURTAIN IS NECESSARY FOR THE ELEGANT FOLDS.

◁

SHEERS CAN LOOK GOOD WHEN USED INFORMALLY IN GENEROUS QUANTITIES. HERE, LENGTHS OF FINE WHITE MUSLIN OVER A POLE REACH DOWN TO THE FLOOR, THEIR BEAUTIFUL SHADOWED FOLDS CONTRASTING WITH SWEEPS OF LIGHT. ALTHOUGH THE EFFECT IS CREATED FROM SEPARATE PIECES, IT APPEARS AS ONE COMPLETE SHEET OF FABRIC.

There are generally two reasons for lining a curtain or shade: to protect the fabric from the light, and to provide extra weight and body.

Over a long period, sunlight, dust and day-to-day wear and tear will do severe damage to a fabric, causing general fading and eventual disintegration. Although most furnishing fabrics should be color- and light-fast, fading does sometimes occur, especially where a curtain or shade is exposed to bright sunlight. If a curtain is lined, it is the lining fabric – whether traditional sateen or some other material – that is exposed to such damage rather than the more expensive main fabric. Traditionally, light-colored linings have been used, notably cream, white or ecru: these light colors will allow some light and heat to pass back through the window.

Attaching a lining has another practical function: it encloses all the hems and raw edges which naturally form during the course of making a curtain or shade, leaving only a neatly turned edge visible. At the base of a curtain the lining will be hemmed and attached along the hem line by loose "daisy chains". These are chains of stitches, each 1–2 inches (2.5–5cm) long, made between the curtain hem and the lining 12 inches apart. The side hems of curtains, and of some shades, are slipstiched by hand. The headings are usually encased beneath a curtain tape or, if the headings are hand-sewn, a strip of thin muslin.

Swags, tails and valances should be lined – unless you deliberately decide to omit the lining in order to achieve a particular effect. There are also some curtains that by their very nature should be unlined: into this category fall sheers, muslins and other lightweight cloths that are intended to filter light rather than block it.

There may also be a purely visual aspect to the use of linings. The basic cotton sateen lining is available not only in creams and ivories but in many different colors besides. Colored linings will affect the color of the fabric in front, unless it is very dense in weave or color. Colored sateens are useful, adding a touch of color when the fabric is draped back to make tails whose linings are revealed. Linings may be taken around the front of a curtain edge, to form a contrast border against the main fabric.

A patterned and plain fabric may be used together, one for the lining and one for the front. Curtains that are seen from the back as much as from the front (for example, bed drapes or curtains on swing arms) can make use of colored or contrast linings. Self-lining is, of course, another option.

"Blackout" linings, not necessarily black, can partially or completely block out light, depending on which type you use. They will make the main fabric rather opaque, which is not especially attractive. However, for some people, the ability to block light completely – in a bedroom, for example – is a worthwhile characteristic.

Thermal lining (milium), which blocks light to a lesser degree, is specially constituted to act as an insulator. It can be used in the same way as any other lining fabric.

Interlining curtains can also make a considerable contribution to the retention of heat within a room and the exclusion of drafts from the window. Interlining (sometimes referred to as "bump") involves the insertion of a soft blanket-like layer of cloth between main fabric and lining. This is sewn under the side and base hems of the curtain and secured with large, loosely formed stitches, across the entire width of the curtain, at intervals of 18 inches (half a meter) or so. This process, called "locking in", allows for the interlining to be attached to the fabric and the lining to the interlining so that the fluid movement of the curtain is not affected, and curtain, interlining and lining move as one. Interlining gives the curtain more body, making it appear fuller and more luxurious – provided that it is fronted by appropriate fabric. It can also help the curtain to drape, softening the folds as the curtain falls.

Weights are essential for making the curtain hang evenly. Even curtains that are intended to bunch onto the floor will stay in place more reliably if they have weighted hems. The weights can take the form of lead disks inserted into the hem, concealed in the turnings and inside their own individual pockets of fabric. They can easily be removed for cleaning. Insert them into each corner and every 12 inches (30cm) or so across the hem.

Another kind of weight, used in muslin or sheer curtains, takes the form of continuous lines of tiny "chainweight", bought by the meter and cut to size. They are threaded into the hem and secured by a few stitches at intervals so that they cannot slip about.

△

IN THIS HIGHLY DECORATIVE ARRANGEMENT WITH SHAPED LAMBREQUIN, THE CONTRASTING PLAIN LINING IS DISPLAYED AT THE WAIST AND FOOT OF EACH CURTAIN. PIPED AND PADDED EDGES FORM A TRANSITION BETWEEN THE LINING AND THE STRIPED MAIN FABRIC.

▷

CO-ORDINATING BED DRAPES AND WINDOW CURTAINS REVEAL A DOUBLE-SIDED EFFECT THAT DEPENDS ON THEIR STYLE OF HANGING. THE LININGS, MATCHED TO THE WALLPAPER, CONTRAST IN PATTERN WITH STRIPES IN THE SAME PALE BLUE. OBSERVE THE REVERSAL OF EMPHASIS: AT THE WINDOW THE DOMINANT ELEMENT IS THE STRIPES, WHILE ON THE BED THE DOTTED PATTERN IS MOST PROMINENT.

It is the heading that largely defines the style of a curtain and, along with the fabric itself, creates the primary impact.

Elegant, hand-sewn French pleating will allow a curtain to fall in graceful yet disciplined folds. Cased headings are more informal, and can suit almost any type of window from large sash to tall, narrow casement. Pencil pleats, too, will go almost anywhere, although they are at their best beneath valances or swags where they are not necessarily on show: they are perhaps the most functional of all headings.

For a touch of grandeur, choose goblet pleats – hand-sewn "tubes" created at intervals across the top of the curtain, stuffed with a brightly colored or otherwise contrasting fabric. This type of heading best suits a pair of curtains that will remain drawn at the top, with the lower part caught with tie-backs, as only then is the full effect of the "goblets" realized.

When you are hanging more than one type of curtain at a window, the choice of heading is even more crucially important. The main curtain, at the front, perhaps crowned by a valance, will be the one that you wish to create the most impact. This front "layer" will carry the design theme of the entire room. The next layer may just be an extension of the first – an elaborate "lining" in the form of a fixed dress curtain barely visible beneath the main one. Its heading may therefore be less important – merely a method of holding the curtain to its own separate rod. Finally, sheer muslin curtains, hung against the window and perhaps intended never to be drawn back to the sides, would require a practical heading – a simple casing – to hang from a lightweight pole.

CASED (OR ROD-POCKET) HEADINGS

This type of heading conceals all but the finials of the pole it is hanging on. The heading is not designed to be physically drawn across the window. Instead, the curtains are held off the window by means of tie-backs: once these are removed, the curtains simply swing across the window, covering the glass. Because it keeps part of the curtains permanently across the window, this type of heading may make the room a little dark. However, it is a very good treatment for muslin or other sheer curtains.

The cased heading does not require tape or hooks. The fabric is simply folded in a band at the top and hemmed with two parallel lines of stitching, which secure the two layers of fabric (or fabric plus lining) and form a "case" or "pocket". This must be wide enough to accommodate the pole or rod you are using, in a fairly snug fit. When calculating the length of the curtain material, remember to add about half an inch (1-2cm), as the curtain will "lift" around the pole. The ruffle that forms above the upper row of stitching at the top of the pole can vary in depth depending on the effect you require. A particularly deep ruffle may need some stiffener to keep it sharp and upright.

GATHERED HEADINGS

These are very loosely pleated headings. They need not be especially full, and will suit informal curtains. When pulled up, a one-inch (2.5cm) tape, placed about two inches (4-6cm) down from the top of the curtain, will form a crisp ruffle of fabric above and very loosely gathered pleats below.

Gathered headings should be used for lightweight or sheer fabrics, and are more suitable for sill-length curtains than for those that fall to the floor. Avoid using this type of heading on heavy fabrics or on particularly weighty curtains, as the narrow tape will be insufficient to hold the weight. Interlining may sometimes be inserted between fabric and lining at the top of this type of heading, to give additional firmness. The strip of interlining should not extend below the lower line of the tape.

PENCIL PLEAT HEADINGS

Curtain tapes have to a large extent replaced hand-sewn headings for curtains. It is extremely rare to find hand-pleated pencil pleats, especially when a curtain tape will do perfectly well.

Pencil pleats are so called because of the narrow pencil-like vertical folds, formed when the pulled tape gathers the curtain into the heading. Pencil pleat tape is usually 3 inches (8cm) deep, although there are other kinds of tape available which form a heading 4–5 inches (10–13cm) deep. The tape comes in different weights – suitable for lightweight, sheer fabric, or heavy velvet or linen. It has three rows of pockets for positioning the hooks, unlike the one-inch tape which has only one row.

Especially deep pencil pleat headings, for very long curtains, require two rows of tape, one placed above the other. Align the pleats carefully, or you will be unable to tighten the heading.

FRENCH PLEAT HEADINGS

This type of heading (also known as a pinch pleat heading) appears as a row of hand-sewn pleats in groups of three separated by flat areas. The entire heading is stiffened with thick fabric such as buckram before the pleating is done: this keeps the heading neat and regimented. There are tapes that will pleat the heading for you, but these are not very satisfactory as they easily sag. French pleats work best when the curtains are interlined, as this adds extra fullness.

The heading must be carefully divided into pleats and spaces so that it will fit neatly and symmetrically into your hanging space. There must be an overlap allowance at the center and a "return" to the wall or window frame at either end; these are both flat unpleated areas of the heading. A pleat should sit on each end of the rod or pole. All the way across the heading, the spaces between the pleats should be the same. For each pleat, a single large "tuck" is made, and then this is divided into a triple pleat, which you secure by hand.

The heading is secured to the curtain pole or rod by means of hooks with large prongs (pin-hooks) which are placed in the curtain at the back of each pleat.

GOBLET PLEATS

These are calculated and formed in the same way as French pleat headings, but instead of making the single tuck or fold into a triple one, you secure only the base of it, forming a short cup. This cup is then stuffed with a rolled-up piece of interlining or Dracon (synthetic filling fiber) to pad out the full shape. A piece of colored lining or contrasting fabric is then inserted at the top and secured with a few stitches. You can make a border at the top of the curtain fabric before you complete the heading, so that when the pleating is finished a neat line defines the sculpted shapes.

SMOCKED HEADINGS

This is a particularly decorative heading, and one that requires a lot of time and careful sewing. The pleats are formed like pencil pleats, either by hand or using a tape. The heading should be fully interlined, as the effect requires considerable padding to look good. The smocked area, on the front of the curtain, needs plotting out first on paper. You then transfer this pattern to the curtain heading, and draw the pleats together at the required points, securing them to each other with stitching.

FLEMISH HEADINGS

A Flemish heading takes the form of goblet pleats linked along their base by hand-sewn cord. The heading should be lined and interlined and stiffened with buckram, as with French or goblet pleats. At their base the pleats should be as narrow as possible: thus, you should use strong thread to catch them in tightly and securely. The cord, knotted at each pleat, should be sewn to the heading along a chalked guideline drawn along the base of the pleats.

Any curtain that incorporates goblet pleats is difficult to draw back without causing the heading to bunch. For this reason, Flemish headings are best used on curtains that remain closed across the top of the window at all times, their lower parts pulled back by tie-backs to let in maximum light.

As an attractive variation, the cord may be secured just at the base point of each pleat rather than all the way across, thus allowing it to loop down when the curtain is drawn back. Again, movement would be restricted. The same approach could be tried with French pleats instead of goblet pleats.

▽

DRAMATIC GOBLET PLEATS ARE GIVEN FURTHER DECORATION WITH DOUBLE LOOPS OF CORDS, ATTACHED TO THE BASE OF EVERY THIRD PLEAT. A GOBLET PLEAT HEADING BEST SUITS A PAIR OF CURTAINS INTENDED TO REMAIN DRAWN AT THE TOP, WITH THE LOWER PART OF THE CURTAINS CAUGHT WITH TIE-BACKS.

▽▽

THESE EXQUISITELY SMOCKED HEADINGS ON BOTH THE OUTER AND INNER CURTAINS OF A BAY WINDOW COMPLEMENT THE ROOM'S INTRICATE ACANTHUS-LEAF MOLDING.

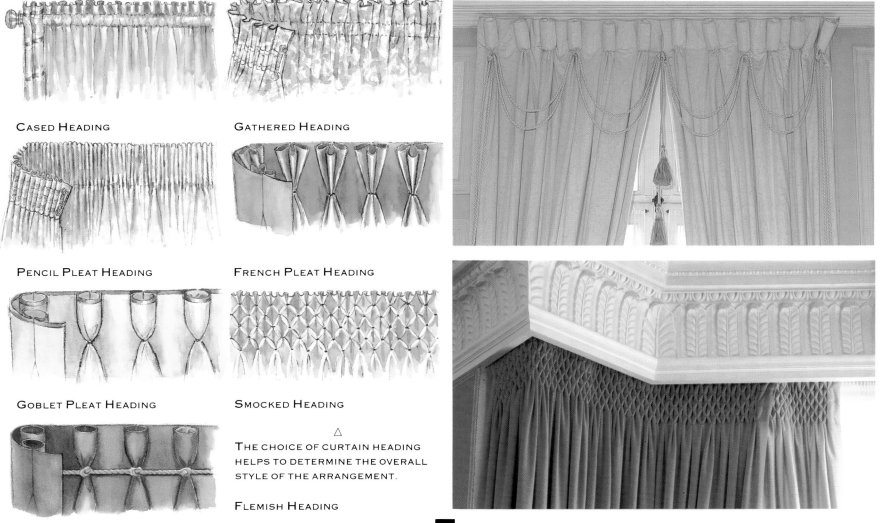

CASED HEADING

GATHERED HEADING

PENCIL PLEAT HEADING

FRENCH PLEAT HEADING

GOBLET PLEAT HEADING

SMOCKED HEADING

△

THE CHOICE OF CURTAIN HEADING HELPS TO DETERMINE THE OVERALL STYLE OF THE ARRANGEMENT.

FLEMISH HEADING

Swag draperies make a fine crown for a curtain, helping to frame the window and the view beyond. In a formal setting they can be highly elaborate constructions. They range from the single full swag, with carefully aligned folds, to multi-layered scoops of fabric decorated with braids and fringes.

In most cases, swags and tails consist of a number of discrete elements, each made separately. Once these components are fitted together, however, the effect is of one piece of "flowing" fabric. This makes a particularly impressive impact when several swags are hung across one wide window.

To outline the individual shape of swags or tails, you can use braids and trims or flat fabric borders. Borders can also be run along the top of the swags, between cornice board and ceiling. If you do not wish each element to be individually emphasized, use one fabric throughout, including areas where the underside of a tail or swag is visible.

Contrast or patterned linings, used sparingly, can define the scoop of a swag or sharpen the shaped edge of tails, without overdefining the separate elements. This approach is especially effective on a large expanse of window where plain, and perhaps light-colored, fabric is used throughout. When you opt for a more decorative arrangement, with several overlapping layers of swags (perhaps in front of a gathered valance), you should resist the temptation to layer too many contrasting fabrics. It is all too easy to overdo things, creating a composition that is cluttered rather than elegant.

The essential ingredient of success is to calculate fabric accurately. Above all, do not skimp. A potentially beautiful arrangement of swags and drapes can be totally ruined by ill-proportioned tails. As a general rule of thumb, take tail lengths at least half-way down the curtain drop, if not further. Swags should fall

some way between one-fifth and one-sixth of the overall drop. However, you can drop them longer or shorter to create a particularly dramatic or luxurious look, or a more linear one. It is also important to consider the proportions across the width as well as down. Overlapping swags should fit comfortably within the window space and not look cramped.

Swags and tails can be fitted to cornice boards, by concealed tacks or staples. The board may be an entirely functional structure concealed beneath fabric folds. Alternatively, cornice boards may be of elaborately carved wood, designed for maximum elegance. The fixtures, in either case, should be hidden – from inside and outside the house.

Loose drapes begin as unshaped lengths of fabric, lined or unlined. Their shape around or above the window is determined according to how the fabric is draped – usually over a pole. Folds form as you manipulate the length around the pole and allow it to fall gracefully to the floor. Fabric can bunch onto the floor, either side of a window, or asymmetrically. If the ends of the fabric are cut diagonally, a tailed effect will form once the fabric is hung. Again, colored linings can be very effective – especially if the material winds around the pole several times. The underside, or lining side, will then be glimpsed between layers of the front fabric. If the drape is not fixed permanently to the pole, the whole thing can be flipped over any time you like, changing the color emphasis. Similarly, several separate lengths can be draped around the same pole for a luxurious yet still informal effect.

Poles for loose drapes need to extend sufficiently beyond the window to prevent it from being too much obscured by fabric. As much of the pole will be concealed, make the most of decorative finials and brackets. If you think you must secure the fabric, the pole must be wood so that tacks can be driven in.

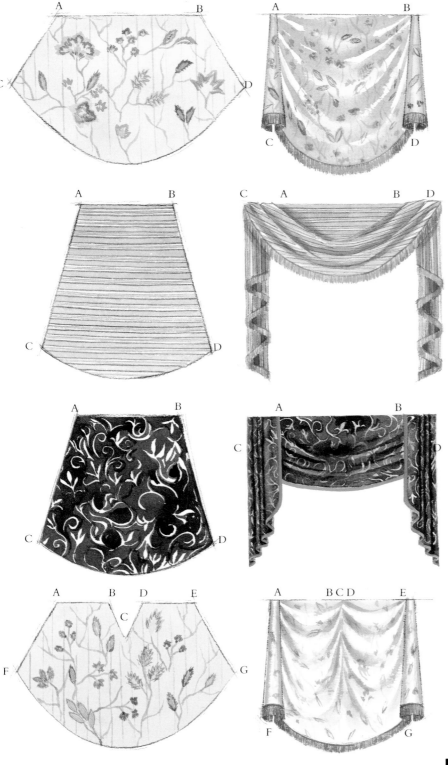

Basic Swags

The illustrations (left) show four different arrangements of swags and tails, all essentially very simple. The second column of diagrams shows the finished appearance of the composition. The first column shows the basic shapes of material used for the swags (not to scale); the tails are all separate components. When making the swags, you should cut the fabric on the bias, as this helps to create natural-looking folds. Interlining may be used on soft fabrics for a fuller effect, but should be avoided with heavy cottons and velvets. Staple or tack the finished pieces firmly to a curtain pole or cornice board.

In the top example, the width of the fabric (A–B) should be 1½× the finished width of the swag.

In the 2nd example, the width of the fabric (A–B) should be half the finished width of the swag. The length of the fabric should be 2–2½× the finished drop of the swag.

In the 3rd example, the width of the fabric (A–B) should be half the finished width of the swag. Again, the length should be 2–2½× the finished drop of the swag, which should be ⅙ or ⅛× the finished drop of the curtain.

In the bottom example, both the width and the length of the V-shaped indent should be ⅓× the finished drop. The width of the fabric (F–G) should be twice the finished width of the swag.

A Tie-back Swag

By controlled use of the tie-backs you can shape a pair of curtains so that they divide naturally into a swag above each tie-back, and a tail below. Attach rings for the cord on a diagonal line along the back of each rectangular piece of curtaining fabric, as shown in the diagram above, left. The diagram above shows both the back and front views of the finished curtain.

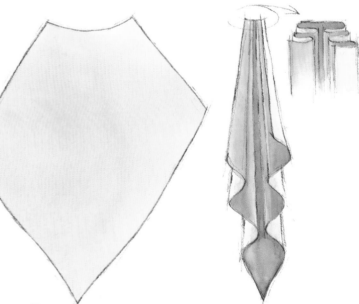

△

SWAGS, OVERLAPPED AND PINNED BY A ROSETTE FOR SUBTLE ASYMMETRY, ARE OFFSET BY A BOX-PLEATED PELMET IN PINK — REPEATED IN THE TAIL LININGS AND ROSETTE EDGINGS.

△

PLAIN WHITE COTTON LINED ON THE TAILS IN A STRONG BLUE CHECK REMAINS STARTLINGLY SIMPLE, DESPITE OVERLAPPING SHAPES. THE KNIFE-PLEATED ROSETTES ADD FOCAL POINTS.

△

THIS COMPOSITION, SET IN A BAY WINDOW, AIMS FOR DRAMA. THE WINDOW HAS A BUILT-IN STRUCTURE FOR SWAGS AND TAILS — THERE WAS NO NEED FOR A SPECIAL FRAMEWORK.

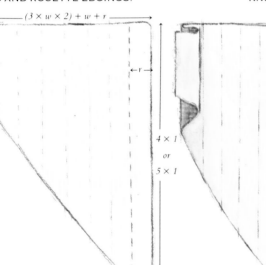

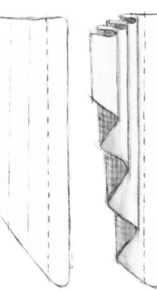

SIMPLE SIDE TAIL

Even to make a simple side tail like this demands care in calculating the amount of fabric. Work from a paper template which you can use for both sides. Take seam allowances into account.
Calculate the width according to this

formula: (number of folds × width of fold × 2) + 1 width of fold + 1 width of return for pelmet. The short vertical edge should be ⅕ to ⅛× the complete tail length.

ASYMMETRIC TAIL

This slightly more complicated tail can be used at either side of a swag, or in the center of the curtaining between swags. Use a paper template cut to the five-sided shape shown above. The edges of the fabric are brought to the

center to create the folds, as shown in the diagram.

NEAT SWAGS WITH TAILS CREATE A COMPACT ARRANGEMENT. THE BLENDING OF THE MARBLED FABRIC GIVES AN IMPRESSION OF OVERALL SHAPE RATHER THAN OF SEPARATE ELEMENTS.

THE STRIPED FABRIC USED HERE IS COMBINED WITH A DIFFERENT STRIPED FABRIC LINING THE TAILS. A FRINGE PROVIDES A TACTILE ELEMENT. LOOPED CORDS SERVE AS A TRIM.

PLAIN SWAGS AND A TAIL ARE SET AGAINST A DEEP STRIPED VALANCE. ALTHOUGH FUSSY AND SOMEWHAT SELF-CONSCIOUS, THE COMPOSITION NEVERTHELESS MAKES AN EYECATCHING FEATURE.

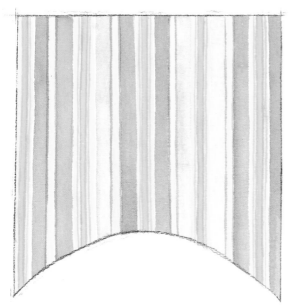

PIPE TAIL

This usually finishes level with or slightly shorter than the swag or pelmet. The template is a rectangle with a curve cut out of it. The width of the rectangle is 3× the finished tail width. The main fabric and the lining

are cut to shape and sewn, separately, to make two open-ended sleeves. These are sewn right sides together along the top edge and the lined tail is then turned out to the finished shape (above). A fringe may be added on the lower edge.

SPIRAL TAIL

The measurement around the curve should be roughly 6× the finished width of the tail at its widest point. The long straight side represents the finished drop. After being cut to shape, the fabric is rolled around its "axis".

FLUTED TAIL

This is a simple tail to use in a pair with a deep swag, as shown on page 131 (left, top and second diagrams). The long edges are not actually joined in this example, but turned so that they just meet.

A SIMPLE IDEA FOR SHEER FABRIC

This arrangement works particularly well with muslin or a similar fine, translucent fabric, but can equally well be used with medium-weight fabrics. A complete length measuring a little more than twice the drop of the window is draped across the pole so that both ends bunch a little at floor level. The front piece is then pulled back and caught to one side by a tie-back – in this example, a plaited one, whose strong color accent contrasts effectively with the flimsiness of the drape. As with most of the arrangements shown on these pages, the forces of gravity acting in balance will sometimes be enough to hold the drapes in place, but some kind of fixing is often desirable. A strip of Velcro tape (or individual patches of tape) tacked along the top of the pole is one option, but this will tend to damage flimsy fabric when you remove it for washing. Using one or two tacks or staples is another way to fix fabric to pole.

ONE STAGE FURTHER

This idea is similar to the one illustrated alongside (left) but goes one stage further: the rear "curtain" is pulled back at a different level from the front curtain to create an effect of asymmetry. The composition uses not one piece of fabric, but two, joined by a concealed seam which lies along the line of the pole. The curtains are pulled back not by tie-backs but by brass rosettes. These consist of pegs, each with a detachable ombra (decorative disk); the sharp end of each peg is pushed into the window frame, leaving around 4 or 5 inches (10–13cm) around which to hook the drapes. The disks may be either ornate, or very plain; it is worth looking around for antique ones, which will fit onto modern pegs without difficulty. The borders appear along the front edges only. Each border could consist of one piece of fabric sewn in place along the edge; or you could assemble your own striped borders from individual pieces.

PERFECT SYMMETRY

Both ideas above show one piece of fabric with contrast lining wound around the pole to create an effect of bulk. The twisted section of the fabric should be twice the pole length. The fabric is first folded in half to find the center, which is marked with a pin. Then you turn the fabric around the pole, starting from one end. To use this arrangement as a frame for curtains behind, leave plenty of space for the rod, and fasten the fabric at crucial points.

AN ILLUSION OF CONTINUITY

This composition creates the illusion that only one piece of fabric has been used. There are actually two separate pieces – a curtain (made to the usual fullness and length, plus some bunching on the floor) held off the window; and a swag with a draped tail, again to floor level. Bobbled fringing along the leading edges will help to strengthen the shape of the composition and make the swag stand out from the curtain. The curtain can be fixed permanently in position, either stapled or tacked to the wooden pole. However, a more flexible option is to make the left-hand element in the illustration a functional curtain, on its own rod behind the pole: it could then be drawn across to cover the entire window. Even if the curtain is fixed, you could unloosen the tie-back and allow the fabric to fall, but in that case you would have to anchor the curtain farther over to the right, closer to the draped tail, to avoid an unwanted gap.

REVEALING HALF THE POLE

Part of the pole can be revealed to create an air of informality. The composition here can be achieved in two different ways. One way is to drape one piece loosely over the pole, using tacks or staples to make sure that the composition is not pulled taut. The other way is to use three separate pieces of fabric: the waisted drape, cut on the diagonal to form a tail at the floor end; the long tail, with an allowance of 5–10 inches (15–25cm) for bunching on the floor; and the swag itself. Obviously, this design works best when the pole is attractive in itself. A black pole can look particularly stylish, especially if the finials are brass.

CLASSICAL BEAUTY

A single length of fabric can be draped over a simple pole symmetrically. The pole may be entirely hidden by fabric (top), or the central portion may be revealed (above). The length of fabric required is twice the drop, plus 1½× the width, with an allowance for bunching if necessary. If you use a contrast lining, you can turn the fabric over from time to time to reverse the colors. Wrapping each drape around the pole again will secure the fabric sufficiently.

△

A DECORATIVE POLE, WITH DIAGONAL BANDS
CROSSING AT INTERVALS, SERVES NOT ONLY AS
SUPPORT, BUT ALSO AS AN ARCHITECTURAL
"FRAME", CONTAINING THE SOFT DRAPES.

▷

A SIMPLE POLE IN DARK WOOD, WITH ROUNDED
DOORKNOB-STYLE FINIALS, IS USED TO PROVIDE
JUST THE RIGHT BALANCE FOR THE FRINGED
FABRIC OF THIS GRAPHIC DESIGN.

△

The means by which a curtain is hung – whether at a window or doorway or around a bed – will make all the difference to the overall effect. Whether intended to be seen or not, the fixing method – pole or rod – must be carefully considered. Often it will predetermine the way in which the curtain or bed-drape will hang.

If the curtain heading is to be on show, as an important *visual* element of the composition, the means by which it is hung and displayed must be treated with the same emphasis.

A pole may well be the most suitable treatment. Poles come in a variety of sizes and finishes – including brass, pine, gunmetal steel and reeded teak. Different fittings are available to suit different situations. Finials, the decorative additions which fit onto pole ends, may be subtle and subdued or generously ornate.

Curtain rods, unlike poles, are designed to be functional. Their role is simply to secure the curtain and, if the rod is corded, to provide the means of operation. Because tracks do not have any interesting visual element to offer, they are used to hold curtains that will hang behind a valance or disguised by swags and tails – that is, designs where the curtain heading is hidden.

Rods can be curved to fit bow or bay windows, so that the curtains can follow their exact contour. It is here that they come into their own, performing a function that is difficult to achieve with poles. Curved rods need to be fitted by a professional curtain fitter.

Poles come in various diameters, from the chunky cornice pole to the slim café rod. Café rods, without rings and usually of brass, may be used for curtains with cased headings. They fit neatly into confined areas – for example, across the middle of a sash window. Special brackets secure the pole and at the same time conceal its

ends. They can be "face-fixed" or "end-fixed"; the latter method can be useful for narrow, recessed areas. These ringless poles can also be used to hold small curtains, top and bottom, *behind* glass – for example, in cupboard doors. Café rods can also be slotted through scalloped headings, forming the café curtains to which they owe their name.

Cornice poles, usually 1⅜-1½ inches (35-38mm) in diameter, are used, with rings, for more substantial curtains, whether floor length or not. They come in standard lengths, which

▽

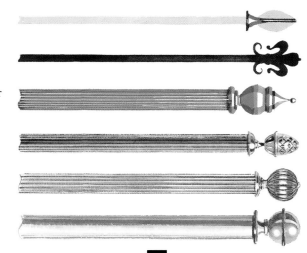

can be shortened. For unusually wide windows, two or three pieces must be joined to the required length. Standard brackets are usually supplied with the pole: however, architrave brackets, which have a slimmer fitting and can thus be fitted onto a narrow vertical beading around the window, may be more suitable. For a contrasting effect, you can use a wooden pole with brass brackets, and perhaps also with brass finials. This not only has visual impact, but may also be useful at a practical level: fabric over wood can easily be tacked or stapled in place.

Finials, bought separately, add a decorative touch, often conjuring up the grandeur of the past. The choice includes spear ends, brass flutes and ornately turned finials in wood.

Rods are usually white plastic or metal. Metal rods, corded and with central overlaps, are recommended: usually telescopic and available in several sizes, they are much stronger than their plastic counterparts. The rod, brackets and fittings are usually supplied complete, but additional fitments can be bought – for example, longer brackets which will support the track at a greater distance from the window or wall, in order to clear a radiator or similar fixture.

Rods should ideally be corded, so that the curtains are handled as little as possible. The cords can be secured around a pulley, which is usually fitted to the baseboard, so that the cords themselves remain hidden behind the curtain. Decorative drop weights can be fitted to the cord ends for an individual touch.

A fascia board can be made to conceal the main part of the rod. This is like a miniature cornice – a 2-inch (5cm) strip of painted or fabric-covered wood fixed along the bottom edge of a cornice board so that it covers the rod.

CORNICES, VALANCES AND LAMBREQUINS

△

HIGHLY ORNAMENTED CORNICES, WITH DOWNWARD-POINTING TRIANGULAR PENNANTS OF ALTERNATING SIZE, ARE THE KEY FEATURE OF THIS ARRANGEMENT FOR A CHINESE DRAWING ROOM (1793). THE TRIANGLES ARE EMPHASIZED BY BORDERS, CENTRAL MOTIFS AND TINY BELLS.

▷

A MEDIEVAL TOURNAMENT PAVILION IS THE INSPIRATION FOR THIS CORNICE IN STRIKING COLORS. CAREFUL EXECUTION ENSURED THAT ALL POINTS AND STRIPES ARE IN PERFECT ALIGNMENT. THE FABRIC, IN JOINED PIECES, FITS OVER A STIFFENED TEMPLATE.

Cornices, valances and lambrequins can be, quite literally, the crowning glory of a curtain arrangement. Positioned at the top of the window, they fit neatly over curtain headings, entirely concealing from sight any rods or fitting mechanism.

Cornices are usually made of wood or a stiffening material such as buckram. Usually they are covered in fabric, but wooden ones may be painted. Valances are made entirely of fabric (which may be lined and interlined). Lambrequins, which are rather like elaborate, extended cornices reaching far down each side of the window, have to be made of wood to retain their boxed shape; set in front of the curtains, they enclose a large proportion of the window itself. All three have the effect of defining the curtain arrangement and linking it with the architectural lines of the window. As well as serving a visual purpose, they can help to eliminate drafts.

Valances create a softer effect than cornices. The heading can be any of those already described for curtains – perhaps a French pleat heading for tall, elegant windows, or a softer, gathered heading for less formal arrangements. A valance can be attached to the edge of a timber board positioned like a shelf above the curtain rod: indeed, the rod is often fitted to the underside of this board. Alternatively, the valance may be hung from a special valance rod hooded onto the main curtain rod. Cased headings can be fitted over a curved valance rod, specially designed to project forward from the curtain.

Cornices are especially useful as a way to outline a window that has a distinctive shape. For example, Gothic windows take shaped cornices very well. Not least of the advantages of a shaped cornice or valance is that it allows you to conceal a straight curtain rod to create a more interesting effect.

MEASURING AND CONSTRUCTION

The board to which the cornice or valance is attached is fitted above and extends to either side of the curtain rod. If this board has the rod attached, it should be fitted level with the top of the window architrave. If the rod is fitted on the window frame itself (for example, where the frame projects unusually far from the wall), the board may have to be fixed to the wall *above* the window. It can be fitted on brackets, evenly spaced and strong enough to hold the weight of the cornice or valance. Of course, if the curtain rod is attached to the board, the brackets have to be strong enough to hold the entire curtain arrangement.

To determine the length of the board, measure the distance the curtain rod will cover, and add at least 2 inches (5cm) at each end. This is to allow for the brackets and to make sufficient space for the curtains to "return" to the wall or the window frame at each end of the rod. You may want the cornice or valance to extend much further than the curtain rod, in which case lengths must be adjusted accordingly.

The drop for a cornice or valance depends on the proportion of the window and the length of the curtains. As a guide, the maximum cornice drop should be approximately one-sixth of the overall drop of the curtain arrangement.

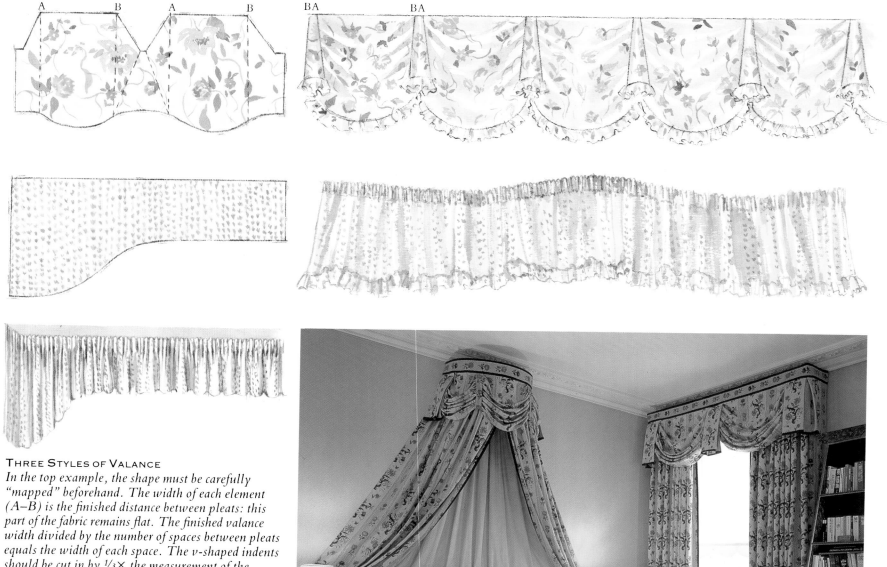

THREE STYLES OF VALANCE

In the top example, the shape must be carefully "mapped" beforehand. The width of each element (A–B) is the finished distance between pleats: this part of the fabric remains flat. The finished valance width divided by the number of spaces between pleats equals the width of each space. The v-shaped indents should be cut in by $^1/_3\times$ the measurement of the finished drop to the lowest point of the curve. There should always be a pleat on each corner of the finished valance.

A valance with a pleated heading (shown complete, second row, right) can be shaped at the top edge or along the base, or both.

A tailed valance (in the two diagrams above) is less austere than one cut level along the base.

▷

IN THIS CORNICE, SHARP BOX-PLEATED TAILS
CONTRAST WITH SOFTER SWAGS.

Valances are often "tailed" and cornices often have a shaped base: such designs demand special care in calculating the amount of fabric needed. A paper template will make it easier to achieve the right shape. You should always take care not to omit the returning edges from your calculations.

To attach a valance or stiffened cornice to its board, you need to attach a strip of Velcro tape to the narrow front edge and ends of the board. This is then matched up with reciprocal Velcro strips attached to the top edge of the valance or cornice. If the cornice is made of wood throughout, rather than stiffened fabric, fix it to the board with tacks.

Borders can be used with great success on the lower edges of cornices or valances. If both the curtain and the cornice are patterned, a plain border will define the outline effectively. You could use a braid or fringe at the base of the cornice: this should be sewn on by hand to obtain best results.

△
A SHAPED CORNICE IS ARTICULATED BY FLUTED TAILS WITH BOWS. A BORDERING FRILL AND BULLION FRINGE COMPLETE THE EFFECT.
△△
TOP GENTLE FESTOONS FORM A VALANCE IN FLORAL CHINTZ, WITH A TAIL EACH SIDE, ROSETTES AT THE TOP AND A BRAID ALONG THE BASE.

△
ELABORATE RUCHING AND FRILLING IS THE KEYNOTE OF THESE VALANCES. THE CURVED TOP STANDS OUT AGAINST THE DARKER WALL.
△△
TOP THIS VALANCE IS MORE FORMAL. LOOPS OF CORD ECHO THE SWAGS, WHICH ARE BORDERED WITH A PATTERNED FRILL.

△
A FLEMISH HEADING WITH DEEP SWAGS IS HIGHLIGHTED BY DECORATIVE FRINGING, AND BY TASSELS AND LOOPS.

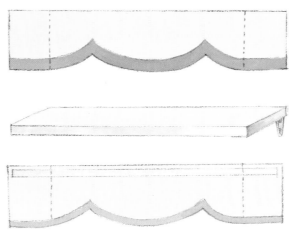

MAKING A CORNICE

Cornices used to be made entirely in wood covered with fabric. Today, a popular method is to use, for the face of the cornice, a template cut in stiffened buckram to the finished dimensions. This must include "returns" to the walls, indicated in the diagrams (left) by dotted lines. The shape is covered with fabric (perhaps bordered) to which a strip of Velcro tape has been sewn along the uppermost edge, as shown in the bottom diagram (rear view). A suitable cornice board (that is, the horizontal part of the cornice) would be a length of 4 × 1 inch (10 × 2.5cm) timber. This is also covered in fabric, and a reciprocal strip of Velcro tape secured along the narrow front and side edges. The board is screwed from underneath into angle brackets fixed to the wall. The fabric-covered cornice is then attached to the board by means of the Velcro tape.

△

A DETAIL OF THE CORNICE IN THE CURTAINING ARRANGEMENT SHOWN ON THE OPPOSITE PAGE. THE SHAPE-DEFINING RED BORDERS AT TOP AND BOTTOM, ORNAMENTED WITH BRAIDING AND MULTI-COLORED TASSELS, TONE WELL WITH THE COLOR OF THE MAIN PATTERN. THE BRAIDING IS EFFECTIVELY REPEATED DOWN THE CURTAIN EDGES.

◁

IN THIS DISPLAY OF RICHLY PATTERNED FABRIC, THE UNUSUAL PRINT HAS BEEN CLEVERLY ALIGNED ON THE CORNICE TO FORM A NEW MOTIF — A RHYTHM OF OVALS, WHICH COMPLEMENTS THE RIPPLING PATTERN DOWN THE CURTAINS. THE VALANCE'S LOWER EDGE HARMONIZES WITH THE GOTHIC MOLDINGS.

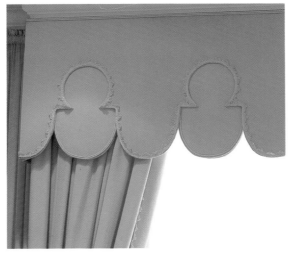

◁

THIS AUSTERE BUT BEAUTIFULLY EXECUTED STIFFENED CORNICE IS CUT OUT WITH KEYHOLE APERTURES, BEHIND WHICH ARE INSERTED ROUNDED SECTIONS THAT HAVE BEEN COVERED IN A TONING FABRIC. THE RESULTING BOTTOM EDGE IS A SERIES OF PERFECT SCALLOPS. A FAN-SHAPED FRINGE DEFINES THE CORNICE'S INTRICATE SHAPE.

▽

THIS FRINGED CORNICE IN A STRIPED FABRIC IS TAILED AT EACH SIDE ACROSS DRAWN-BACK CURTAINS. A MINI-CORNICE ALONG THE TOP EDGE ABUTS A HORIZONTAL STRIPE CHOSEN TO MATCH THE CURTAINS. THE TWO CORNICES SHOWN ALONGSIDE VARY IN DETAIL BUT SHARE THE SAME MOCK-HERALDIC MOOD.

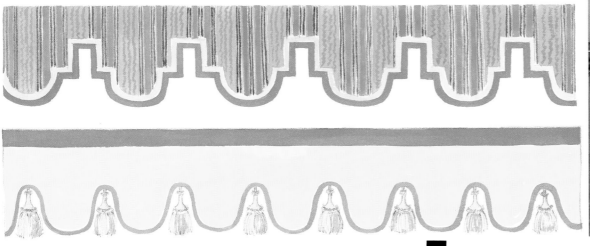

BORDERS, RUFFLES AND TRIMMINGS

Borders help to emphasize shape and form. They can be particularly effective along the leading edges of curtains, along the hem, along the heading, or around the base of a valance either at a window or on a bed-canopy. Tiebacks can be bordered, and shades, especially, can be transformed by this embellishment.

For borders to work well, they need careful planning. Usually, they are made in a fabric or braid that contrasts with the main fabric. A border should complement the fabric to which it is being applied and, even more importantly, it should be consistent with the fabric's shape and style.

Borders may be flat, frilled, pleated or piped. Sometimes several sorts can be used together: for example, although a Roman shade, being flat, could take only a flat border, a balloon shade may be frilled, or piped and frilled, around its edge, or may have a flat border inset into the main fabric.

FLAT BORDERS

Sometimes, you may want a flat fabric border that runs along just one edge of the fabric: for example, along the vertical side of a curtain. If the border is to run along the adjacent *horizontal* edge as well, the two pieces of fabric should meet in a neat, flat miter at the corner. Mitered corners are essential in keeping the fabric flat and the corner accurately right-angled.

Overlapping borders, particularly effective on Roman shades, are a clever way of incorporating two, or sometimes three, additional fabrics. The border fabrics may contrast in color or in texture with the main fabric. Take special care in judging the proportions: for example, an especially wide border on a small shade or curtain would look ridiculous.

A flat border may be assembled from several fabric pieces. To make an interesting contrast on a plain curtain or shade you might choose to

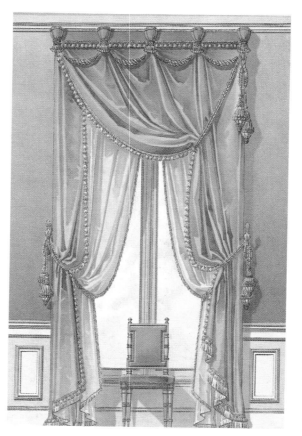

△

make a striped border out of two differently colored fabrics. When a flat border is to be applied to a rounded or shaped edge, perhaps on the edge of a cornice, the fabric should be cut on the bias.

FRILLED BORDERS

Frills are intended to run along the edge of a curtain or shade: for example, the lower edge of a balloon shade. They may be gathered, or pleated, to form sharp folds or knife pleats. Gathered frills are more common and easier to do. The frills, made up separately, are either caught into the seam at the edge of the main fabric or applied over the top of the fabric. They can be self-lined or lined with a contrasting fabric, which can then be taken round the front of the frill edge as a border.

Two to two-and-a-half times the finished length is usually sufficient for an evenly gathered frill. Do not skimp on fabric – frills need to be full. It is usually necessary to join pieces in order to obtain the length required, then the whole piece is folded in half lengthwise, the two raw edges meeting. The frill is then gathered, before being applied to the main fabric.

PIPING

Piping is simply a cord covered in fabric and then applied, for example, to a tie-back or curtain edge. The cord may be encased in one strip of one color, perhaps to contrast with the main fabric. Alternatively, a casing made up of lengths of striped fabric can look particularly good against a plain area. One use for piping, plain or striped, would be between the frilled edge and the main fabric of a balloon shade.

PADDED EDGES

These firm, rounded edges, usually found only on curtains, are made from stuffing rolled into long sausage shapes, and enclosed within fabric

◁

▷

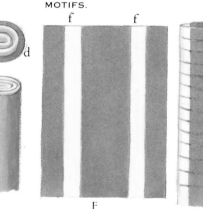

△

A CONTRAST OF DELICATE STRIPED SILK WITH HEAVY TASSELS AND A BULLION FRINGE SWEEPING THE FLOOR. BRAID FINISHES THE CURTAIN'S LEADING EDGE.

△

A DELICATE KNIFE-PLEATED FRILL, CAUGHT BETWEEN MAIN FABRIC AND LINING, EDGES THESE CURTAINS. BEHIND IS AN INNER CURTAIN OF UNLINED SILK.

△

THE MAIN CURTAIN FABRIC HAS SUGGESTED THIS SUITABLE EMBELLISHMENT: A STRIPE FROM THE FABRIC KNIFE-PLEATED AS A BORDERING FRILL.

△

A DOUBLE-BORDERED KNIFE-PLEATED FRILL EDGES THIS CURTAIN, ITS PLAIN GREEN BAND PICKING OUT THE COLORS OF STEM AND LEAF MOTIFS.

borders. The border fabric is already attached to the curtain edge and is secured around the stuffing. Piping can be applied between main curtain and padded edge, as shown in the middle diagram on this page. Often the border and main fabric are the same.

BRAIDS AND FRINGES

There are numerous braids and fringes that can make decorative borders, often lending an antique finish. Bought by the yard or meter, they can be applied to the edges of valances, curtains and some shades. Most of them, particularly fringes hung off the edge of an item, need hand-sewing for a neat finish; and some are just too bulky to fit under the foot of a sewing machine. Flat braids, applied along the edge or set in from the edge of a curtain, can sometimes be machine-sewn. Bobble fringes can be used to create a regular rhythm of accents, rather than a continuous uniform edging.

A selection of braids and trimmings available today is illustrated in the photograph on pages 176–7, ranging from picot braids (with S-shaped edges) to ropes and cords of varying thicknesses.

THREE STYLES OF EDGING

Here are three different approaches to curtain edging.

The first example (A and B) is a broad gathered frill with a border. A strip of flat fabric with the border (a) attached is doubled over, wrong sides together, to make a self-lined fold (A). This is gathered along the edge (b) and applied to the curtain edge right sides together (B). When the frill is folded back, the raw edges are hidden.

The second example (C, D, E) is a padded edge with piping (c) and a border (d). The curtain fabric is laid on a flat surface and interlining (e) placed on

top, overlapping the curtain edge. The interlining is then folded over in a roll and secured beneath the curtain hem. The border is folded around the padding and secured by stabbing stitches. A simpler version of the same method is to omit the piping and the border, as shown in E.

The third type of edging (F and G) is a double-edged knife-pleated frill (top row, fourth photograph). A strip of fabric with borders (f) pieced into it is folded over to make a tube, joined, and then pressed with a very hot iron into regimented strips.

FRINGING IN TWO COLORS OR TONES CAN PROVIDE A LINK BETWEEN THE MAIN FABRIC AND THE LINING IN AN ARRANGEMENT OF TAILS. IN THIS EXAMPLE, THE COLORS HARMONIZE PERFECTLY, CREATING AN ATMOSPHERE OF MELLOWNESS AND WARMTH. FRINGING ALWAYS HAS A SOFTENING EFFECT, AND THUS CAN BE USED TO MODIFY A COMPOSITION THAT MIGHT OTHERWISE SEEM A LITTLE TOO FORMAL.

A BROAD LOZENGE-PATTERNED BORDER IN WARM RED AND SOFT CREAM ATTRACTIVELY OFFSETS RICH PLAIN CURTAINS AT AN ARCHED WINDOW. INVISIBLE TIE-BACKS CAUSE THE CURTAINS TO DRAPE IN SUCH A WAY THAT PARTS OF THE BORDERS, BELOW THE "WAIST", ARE HIDDEN FROM VIEW. THE CURTAIN HEADING HAS A NARROW BORDER IN PLAIN BURGUNDY AND IS FURTHER DEFINED BY A BROAD ROPE IN THE SAME COLOR, DECORATIVELY KNOTTED.

Fabric, cord or ribbon tie-backs are useful ways to enrich a curtain or pair of curtains – provided that you get the proportions right. It is frequently the tie-backs that determine the overall finished form of the curtains. For example, if curtains are hung in a pair so that a generous scoop of fabric forms when they are caught back to the sides of the window, it will be the tie-back that keeps them there, creating the effect of fullness.

The tie-back makes a similar contribution to the presentation when there is just one curtain running across the entire width of the window. By lifting the base of the curtain, the tie-back can be used to create a sort of tailing effect, revealing areas of the lining that can make a contrast with the main fabric.

Tie-backs can be used to scoop the fabric, at intervals, all the way down the curtain, forming deep ruches and creating a very theatrical effect. In such arrangements, tie-backs serve both a practical and decorative role, as they are nearly always on view.

The most effective tie-backs are often the simplest. A long, narrow strip of self-lined fabric, widening out at each end, makes an

excellent tie-back, which can be tied casually around the curtain and allowed to tail to the ground. Or you can make a more exaggerated bow, with the ends of the strip cut diagonally for a neat finish. The "tails" can be just long enough to trail on the floor, or they can just sit within the folds of the curtain. The best way to hold such a tie-back in place is to secure a small brass curtain ring half-way along the untied strip; this is fastened over a hook placed at the side of the window.

Plaited tie-backs are appealing and, if made well, can be fairly formal – almost like a cord. Use surplus fabric from the curtain, and perhaps one or two pieces of contrasting fabric, and make these into three tubes, lined with interlining to give a softer effect. Secure the tubes neatly together at one end, leaving the other ends free. Weight the sewn end on a table, or ask someone to hold it, while you do the plaiting. When you have finished plaiting, secure the remaining ends. The tubes can be exaggerated with more stuffing to form a heavier, more rounded plait; or you can plait flat pieces of fabric – ribbons, for example – to make more delicate tie-backs. Small brass curtain rings, sewn at each end of the

△

IN THIS HISTORIC FRENCH DESIGN, SIMPLE CORD TIE-BACKS WITH TASSELED ENDS SHAPE THE OUTER CURTAINS, WHILE PLAINER STIFFENED BANDS HOLD THE INNER CURTAINS OFF THE WINDOW.

◁

THESE BEAUTIFULLY PATTERNED DAMASK CURTAINS ARE HELD BY ROPE TIE-BACKS, EXQUISITELY COLORED, WITH ELABORATELY TASSELED BAUBLES. THE PLAITS INCORPORATE TWO THICKNESSES OF CORD: TWO THINNER CORDS ARE TWISTED TOGETHER TO MAKE UP PRECISELY THE DIAMETER OF THE THICKER CORD. ROPE TIE-BACKS OF THIS KIND ARE ESPECIALLY SUITABLE FOR ELEGANT PERIOD INTERIORS.

▷

A LARGE FABRIC BOW FINISHES OFF THE GATHERED BAND SECURING THIS CORNER CURTAIN ON A CANOPIED BED. THE BOW CONSISTS OF TWO PIECES OF FABRIC ARRANGED CROSSWISE, WITH A FABRIC-COVERED DISK IN THE CENTER.

PLAITED TIE-BACKS
Plaited fabric tie-backs – an alternative to rope – add textural contrast to the vertical pleats of curtains. You will need three "tubes" of fabric lined with interlining and secured. The ends of each are flattened slightly and hemmed by hand (above left). After you have finished the plaiting and secured the ends, the ring on the front half of the tie-back needs to be hidden by setting it in from the end: the diagram (top right) shows the underside. The ring on the back end of the tie-back can be simply stitched on the edge (above right, center).

◁

MAKING PLAITED TIE-BACKS IN THE SAME FABRIC AS THE CURTAINS IS A GOOD WAY TO USE UP SURPLUS MATERIAL – THE APPROACH TAKEN IN THIS BEDROOM ARRANGEMENT.

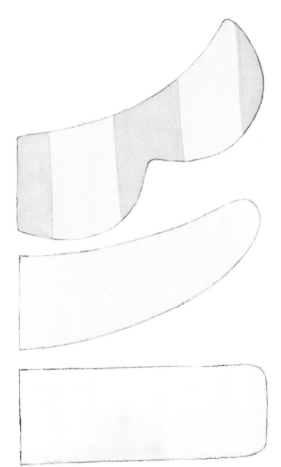

STIFFENED TIE-BACKS

The diagrams above show three different shapes for stiffened tie-backs – that is, those made from a shaped template of stiff material (usually buckram) covered with fabric on both sides, and with a piped edging. The piping is usually of a contrast fabric. The diagram below shows the underside of a stiffened tie-back. The front edge is on the left (note the position of the ring, which has to be hidden from

view when the tie-back is in place). The piping joint is made on the back half of the tie-back, again so that it remains invisible.

finished tie-back, will secure it to the wall hook.

Perhaps the most commonly seen tie-back is one made by covering a shaped template with fabric outlined with piping. These tie-backs are often crescent-shaped, tapering neatly. Most shapes are suitable: you can square the ends, sharpen the curve or flute the lower edge.

The piping may be varied in many ways. Striped fabrics cut on the bias make good edgings; or you can make your own striped fabrics by joining several contrasting strips together, either evenly spaced or arranged more randomly. Striped pipings, with two or three strong contrasting colors, look particularly dramatic on a plain dark-colored tie-back that accompanies a curtain in the same fabric.

Rope or cord tie-backs, made from silk or cotton (or sometimes a combination of both), are perhaps the most formal and grand of all. Even an unbleached cotton rope, with the faintest hint of a tassel, to tie back a plain muslin curtain, can look stunning. Ropes with double ends (tassels at each end) are easiest to tie: fold them in half and thread both ends through the loop formed at the half-way point. For that professional touch, position the tasseled ends so that they lie at different levels on the curtain.

To gauge tie-back lengths, take a tape-measure around the curtain, holding it so that the fabric falls with the desired effect. For example, if you want the curtain to hang loosely, there should be plenty of slack in the tie-back – and correspondingly in the tape-measure. Add two inches (5cm) or so to the final measurement. For rope tie-bands, allow at least twice the amount around the curtain again, for tailing.

Hooks for the tie-backs need to be positioned carefully, in order to display the curtain to best effect and in the optimum proportion to the window. As a rule of thumb, the base of the tie-back should be positioned two-thirds of the way down the window. This does not mean that the hook itself is to be placed at this point. Sometimes the hook will go much higher – especially with rope tie-backs, which hang almost vertically around the curtains.

Metal tie-backs (notably brass) are another option. Fixed to the window architrave or wall, they allow the curtain simply to hook behind them. The type that resemble pegs, protruding from the wall, with a plain or decorative disk, look particularly effective with bed drapes.

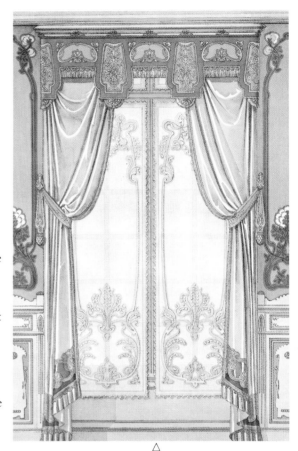

A HISTORIC ARRANGEMENT IN WHICH THE SLENDER FABRIC-COVERED TIE-BACKS, POSITIONED HIGH TO LET IN LIGHT AND SHOW OFF THE PATTERNED SHEER HANGINGS, ARE CONSISTENT WITH THE STYLE OF THE VALANCE. ORNATE BOBBLES CONTRIBUTE A SENSE OF POISE AND WEIGHT.

ROSETTES

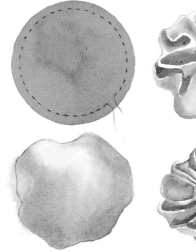

Rosettes, primarily, are devices for focusing attention on a particular area within a curtain arrangement. They can make an attractive "finishing-off" motif for curtain headings, swags and tails, and tie-backs. Of course, the rosettes must be set against a background of suitable fabric, whether in a curtain or as part of a swag arrangement.

Rosettes are made up separately. Often, they employ the same material as is used for the curtains they are embellishing. Alternatively, they may be made from a contrasting fabric – for example, a strikingly dark pattern against a pale cream curtain.

CHOUX ROSETTE

The starting point for this is a circle of fabric 2–3× the diameter of the finished rosette (top left). To "draw in" the material, large tacking stitches are sewn around the circumference ¾inch (2cm) in from the raw edge, and the threads pulled (above left). The folds are secured by concealed stabbing stitches (top right). The raw edges, at the back, are hidden by a fabric-covered disk (above right).

There are three types of rosettes – knife-pleated, choux (ruched) and bow-shaped (or fleur de lys) – all illustrated on this page. The choux is the type which, when complete, projects farthest from the curtain surface. This is the most commonly used type of rosette, and the one that can be made most randomly. It will sit rather like a ruched puff ball, and is best executed in the same fabric as the curtains, although this is not a binding rule.

The knife-pleated and bow-shaped rosettes are more tailored, and consequently require more time and calculation in their construction. The knife-pleated type is made from a length of fabric, pleated and then sewn into a circle. The bow type is cut from a template and the individual flaps or "leaves" are then secured to make the final shape.

All rosettes require a small piece of backing material, such as a piece of stiffener covered with fabric, to enable them to be secured to the curtain or the valance.

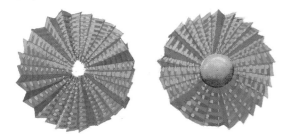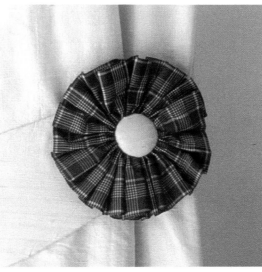

KNIFE-PLEATED ROSETTE

To make a knife-pleated rosette like the tartan one illustrated (above right), you will need a length of fabric three times the circumference of the finished rosette. The fabric is knife-pleated and then turned to form a circle, as shown in the diagram, above left. After the ends have been joined, you need to fill the central hole with a fabric-covered disk, securing it at the back by slip stitching around the edge. The central disk may match the fbric of the rosette, or alternatively you could choose a contrasting plain color, as in this example. It is often effective to use a patterned rosette with a plain disk that matches the curtain fabric.

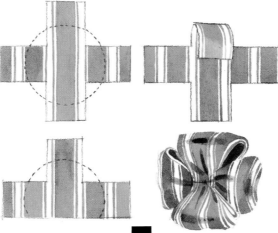

BOW-STYLE ROSETTE

Two pieces of matching fabric are cut to a cross or inverted T, following either of the designs shown in the diagrams, far left (top or bottom). The two pieces are machine-sewn together, right side to right side, leaving a gap along one edge, and the whole is then turned right side out and secured. Then each leaf of the cross or trefoil is folded toward the center (along the dotted lines in the diagrams) so that the ends overlap, gathered along the inner edge, and secured by stabbing stitches. The shape of the leaf section can be varied to give the rosette a "fatter" appearance. The overall effect may be formal or informal, depending on how crisply each segment of the rosette is made.

Bed curtainings are usually most successful when the distinction between the outer fabric, on view from within the room, and the inner, on view from the bed, is highlighted. Working with two equally important sides of fabric in this way is an exciting challenge. Both sides will be on show, especially if the curtains drape around the entire bed, and the two fabrics, if they are different, have to work together. From the room, the "lining" has to act as a backdrop to emphasize the main fabric, outlining the shape and form of the curtains and drapes.

There are several ways to distinguish the outer and inner fabrics so that the juxtaposition of elements – valance, corner drapes, back curtain – does not become confusing. Opposites make the most effective combination – patterned against plain, dark against light. The use of borders to edge the different components can also be successful. Narrow, subtle borders work well – thin stripes of color around pale drapes, or bold stripes on rich, dark silks. Mixing fabric weights and textures in bed curtains can have great impact, forming contrasts that can be further emphasized by whatever fabric covers the bed itself.

The arrangement of bed curtains will depend largely on the style of bed itself, and its position within the room. A four-poster demands rather grand treatment, not necessarily on an opulent scale, but certainly sympathetic with the general style and structure of the bed.

Whether or not the curtains are designed to be drawn, their fixing should be concealed beneath the top wooden frame, or behind a valance. Bed valances need not be stiffened and shaped: a swathe of fabric loosely caught up at intervals to form a series of informal swags can be just as pleasing as more formal treatment. Tails, hanging down at the corners of the bed, will go well with any style of swag.

If you want to simulate a four-poster effect on an ordinary bed, it is not too difficult to make a frame of joined poles. Fabric can be wrapped over the poles, or curtains with simple cased headings hung from them. More simply, a fabric canopy can be created, slung over two parallel poles supported above and across the bed. One pole is fitted against the wall behind the bed head, and the other is suspended half-way down the bed, or across its foot, on brackets fitted to the ceiling. The canopy, essentially just a

▷
MAGNIFICENTLY DRAPED IN MONOGRAMED SILK, THIS CANOPIED BED IS RESPLENDENT IN SHIMMERING COLORS AND YARDS OF FABRIC. THE COVERED PLATFORM IS A SIMPLE YET EFFECTIVE IDEA. NOTE ALSO THE WADDED EDGE IN YELLOW AND THE THREE-COLOR FRINGE.

▽
THIS TREATMENT OF SIMPLE DRAPES AROUND A SUBTLY ORNATE ENGLISH FOUR-POSTER BED IS FROM AN ISSUE OF ACKERMANN'S *REPOSITORY*, PUBLISHED IN 1816. THE BORDERS ON THE DRAPES AND VALANCE ARE SUITABLY RESTRAINED.

rectangle of cloth, encloses the bed in two walls of curtain, with a curving scoop of fabric in between. For a lighter effect, take the fabric only part of the way down at the foot end of the bed, or alternatively finish it at the second pole with a fitted cased heading up against the ceiling.

A half-canopy, whether structural or improvised, offers many options for curtaining. Traditionally, a half-canopy is a bed with an extended frame at the head, usually with a valance, and drapes at either side making a shallow recess. One variation is to sweep back two drapes from the head, with another curtain, flat against the wall, in the triangular space created between the two drapes. Alternatively,

you can run a single curtain symmetrically around the inside of the half-canopy, leaving the front open so that the curtains look like a pair. You can create your own version of a half-canopy using a board projecting from the wall on brackets. Or, more easily, you can fix a pole projecting over the bed head just below ceiling level, with drapes sweeping out from it.

A crown, fixed above the bed, can look very pretty. Usually, crowns are circular, and small in proportion to the bed area – typically, around 30-40 inches (80-100cm) in diameter. From the crown it is usual to have curtains hanging and spreading around the bed like a tent, arranged on upright supports that rise from each of the four corners of the bed. Alternatively, the crown may have just a short cornice, shaped and stiffened, or perhaps loosely draped into swags. Careful calculation is needed to achieve a successful balance between the fabric above the bed and that on or around it.

With any of these arrangements, it is essential to take special care when fixing supports. Before attaching to ceilings and walls, make sure that they will be able to take the strain of heavy fabric and the poles or testers from which they hang. The art of disguise is a crucial ingredient of success: usually, it is desirable to give the impression, almost, that the whole arrangement is supported on an invisible frame.

Braids and trimmings can make any of the above-mentioned effects more dramatic. Tasseled tie-backs can hold curtains off the bed area, or be used in a purely decorative way, hanging from spear-ended poles.

Nowadays, bed curtains are used purely as ornament, rather than fulfilling their original function of insulation. However, you should avoid the temptation to overstress the decorative aspects with too many elements and impractical fastenings or trimmings.

Fabric and trimmings will both attract much dirt, especially on areas that are handled least, where dust gathers. It is thus important that all the separate components can be easily removed for cleaning.

Historic prints, especially those of the early 19th century, will offer an inspiring source of ideas. Usually, you will need to simplify a historic arrangement considerably to make it appropriate to today's requirements, even if the room is a period one.

BED CURTAINS

THE DEEP GATHERED VALANCE ON THIS BED SITS
AGAINST A KNIFE-PLEATED FRILL APPLIED BEHIND
THE VALANCE HEM, WITH A CONTRAST LINING ON
THE INSIDE. THE CORNER CURTAINS, WAISTED BY
CONCEALED TIES, DRAPE JUST TO THE FLOOR.

VALANCE VARIATIONS

*The valance is the element that most determines the
character of a four-poster bed like the one below.
Four different options are illustrated on this page.*

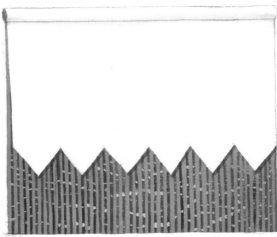

For the valance shown above, a contrast or self-lined
piece of fabric is cut to the finished width (there is no
fullness) and to the drop required plus about 1/3
fullness. The fabric is swagged by tasseled cord tied
around the four-poster frame – a pole threaded
through a cased heading. The valance below, also
case-headed on a pole, is best used with lightweight
fabrics. The fabric ties are secured by stitching at each
side and knotted at the bottom to scoop the fabric.

The design above depends on two contrasting fabrics,
each highlighting the other. The two pieces, one cut
slightly shorter and with a shaped lower edge, are
joined together along their top edge. A cased heading
at the top of the valance fits onto the pole of the bed
frame. The fabric could have fullness across the
width for a more relaxed effect.

Bed skirts look most effective when the fabric is
matched to that of the valance, as in the example
illustrated (left).

A "scooped-up" length of fabric (below) with
supporting rope ties spaced further apart produces a
softer, less formal style. It is important to keep the
ties even in length so that the scoop is level. Wide
braid can be used instead of rope.

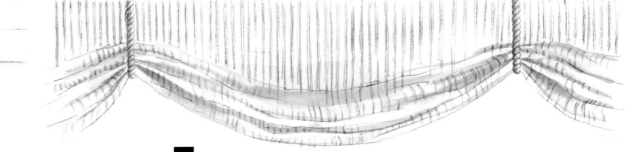

An arrangement of Moorish splendor in a crisp blue and white English cotton print. From a central ceiling-mounted crown (a fabric-covered band around a ring of wood) four unlined lengths of fabric span out to ornate corner posts and then twist once around and down to the floor.

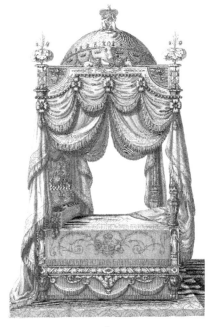

△

A simplified four-poster design of 1793 which allows for one of the posts to be on show. The asymmetry is rather pleasing. Braids and fringes adorn the ornate crown, and the skirt of the bed is treated like a valance, with swags, tails and rosettes.

△

CENTER This arrangement is identical to the one illustrated at the top of the page, but with pyjama stripes instead of dotted flower motifs. The blue is picked out very delicately in the cushions and on the wallpaper, whose simplified pavilion motifs wittily echo the bed arrangement.

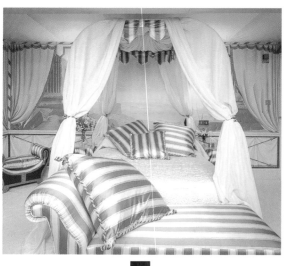

An English four-poster state bed with a magnificent domed crown and cascades of swags and heavy fringed drapes in two layers, creating an effect of enclosure. Rosettes at two different levels help to strengthen the emphasis at the top of the composition.

◁

Floating white drapes over a metal frame form an open tent around this bed in a TROMPE L'ŒIL room. More of the same fabric is loosely pleated from a central point inside the structure, forming a "ceiling". Striped pennants all the way around the inside are revealed in the spaces between the drapes.

BED CURTAINS

▷

BELOW RIGHT THIS HISTORIC DESIGN (1826) USES LONGER POLES FOR A WEIGHTIER EFFECT AND INCORPORATES CONTRASTING LINING THAT IS ON SHOW JUST AS MUCH AS THE MAIN FABRIC.

▽

RICHLY COLORED, IN RED, OCHER AND DEEP BLUE, THE FABRIC OF THIS SIMPLE CANOPY CONTRASTS STRIKINGLY WITH DARK GREEN WALLS AND MATCHES THE CURTAIN ARRANGEMENT. A WOODEN WALL-MOUNTED POLE AND TWO BRASS ROSETTES PROVIDE SUPPORT.

BED CURTAINS

MAKING A CORONET

There are two basic components in a coronet: a disk of timber covered with fabric (right, top diagram); and the cornice (bottom). The disk is cut to size and screw holes are drilled in. It is then covered with fabric and Velcro tape secured along its narrow edge. The covered disk is then fixed to the ceiling. The cornice is made from a strip of stiffened buckram curved and fastened to make a tube. Fabric and lining are then cut and sewn so that this covering can then be slipped over the buckram in one complete piece. Reciprocal Velcro tape is sewn along the top edge of the lining before slotting over the buckram and slip-stitching the open edges: there is usually no need for any other fastening. If the coronet is to be placed against a wall, the cornice should be made as an incomplete circle (third diagram) and the disk shaped with a flat edge to match.

SHAPED CORONETS

The illustrations below show two attractive coronet designs that could easily be made at home. It is always best to experiment on paper before committing your design to the finished piece of buckram.

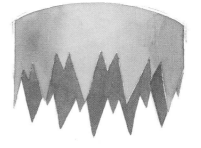

▷

THIS DRAMATICALLY SHAPED CORONET FORMS THE FOCAL POINT IN THE BEDROOM. CURTAINS SWEEP FROM INSIDE THE STRUCTURE DOWN TO EACH CORNER OF THE BED, WHERE EACH IS HELD BY A LARGE CROSS-SHAPED ROSETTE.

▽

BOTTOM LEFT THIS CORONETED BED HAS A GATHERED VALANCE BENEATH A RUCHED BORDER, THE LATTER IN A YELLOW PRINT OF DELICATE PATTERN THAT CONTRASTS WITH THE BOLDER MAIN FABRIC.

▽

A SOFA BED DESIGN OF 1791, WITH A DOMED CORONET SURMOUNTED BY A PLUME OF FEATHERS. THE VALANCE AROUND THE BASE OF THE DOME CONSISTS OF OVERLAPPING SWAGS RESTING AGAINST A PLAIN CORNICE. THE CURTAINS THEMSELVES, IN CONTRASTING PLAIN FABRICS, ARE INTERESTINGLY CAUGHT OVER DOUBLE RINGS ATTACHED TO ORNATE WALL BRACKETS.

ROLLER SHADES

Simple in construction, and plain even to the point of austerity, roller shades are the most functional of all window furnishings. When let down, they fill the window space like sheets of canvas. When rolled up, they sit unobtrusively at the top of the window – a cylinder of fabric, coiled neatly around a wooden, or sometimes metal, roller.

Unlike all other fabric furnishings, these shades do little to exploit the *softness* of fabric. The material you use must be stiffened for the shades to function correctly. This process, usually done industrially, reduces the tactile quality of the fabric. However, this does not detract from the appeal of these shades: after all, it is precisely for their plainness that roller shades are chosen.

Instead of being displayed alone at a window, a roller shade may be used as the "hidden" element of a window dressing. For example, it may serve a functional role behind drapes that are left permanently open as a visual frame for the window. Also, the flatness of this type of shade can be exploited to provide a contrasting surface with the folds of curtains or loose drapes.

In some rooms, particularly kitchens and bathrooms where steam and heat can adversely affect fabric, roller shades can be the most practical form of window treatment. In any case, these are rooms where, for esthetic reasons, a simple, uncluttered effect is usually required.

There are also certain difficult situations where roller shades come into their own – for example, on slanting windows, or on skylights where other furnishing treatments would not be possible. When the window is on a slope, the shade must be fixed at its base when fully down, to hold it against the window. The same problem can be solved by choosing roller shades that operate on a runner system: the shade is attached by rings to runners at either side of the sloping window. Another solution is to slot the roller shade behind poles, which will keep it relatively flat against the slanted glass.

ROMAN SHADES

A Roman shade has all the grace and simple beauty of a sail. Strength and durability are also among its characteristics. The success, in both practical and visual terms, of this clever and modern piece of window furnishing lies mainly in its construction. Operating on a simple

cording system, the Roman shade pulls up into a series of folds, one upon the other. When down, the shade is simply a flat area of fabric covering the window space. The support and weight necessary for keeping the shade neat and the fabric taut come from a number of dowel rods which are secured horizontally – usually across the back, but sometimes along the front, of the shade itself.

Roman shades are somewhat architectural in character, well defined in their angles, and precise in the relationship of one fold to another. The fabric provides an element not so much of texture, but more of flat color, with plenty of possibilities for graphic impact. Thus, a Roman shade works best with non-patterned fabrics, either plain or with simple stripes. The effect you aim for should be free of clutter.

Borders, differing from the main fabric either in their color or in the direction of their stripe, can be added to provide outline and emphasis. When attached to the edges of the main piece of fabric, such borders become an extension of the whole, so that you are dealing with just a single complete piece of fabric when the shade is made up. Another approach is to use inset borders, set in from the sides of the shade. These are treated in the same way as borders attached to the outside edge: that is, they are not applied to the main fabric, but joined to it along the edges, with all the seams and stitch lines on the back of the shade. It is worth mentioning that when the shade is down, with the light behind it, all seams and turnings will be visible: so make sure that all cut edges and stitch lines are straight.

The dowels, contained within pockets made from tucks in the shade fabric, can be of wood or, with particularly lightweight and even sheet fabrics, of plexiglas. They need to be half-round, so that they sit flat against the fabric. Applied dowel pockets positioned on the front of the shade offer a way to add color and contrast. Roman shades can have a pleasantly translucent appearance if left unlined, but mostly they tend to be lined, with the lining applied by hand to the turned-under side hems.

The top of the shade holds a concealed wooden batten from which the fabric hangs. When calculating the length of the shade, you need to add to the intended drop an extra length of fabric for covering this batten. Screw eyes for the cord are fixed underneath.

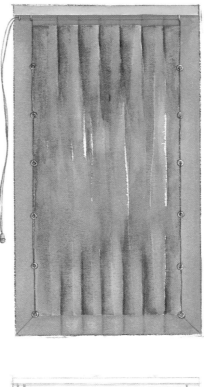

A SINGLE-SCOOP ROMAN SHADE IN SILK
CONTRASTS WITH DARK CURTAINS.

TOP A PLAIN DARK ROMAN SHADE IS SET AGAINST
A COOL, NEAR-MONOCHROME INTERIOR.

CENTER TWO ROMAN SHADES HANG AT THE SAME
WINDOW IN THIS MODERN, BLUE ROOM. ONE
SHADE IS UNLINED, AND CREATES A SHEER
SCREEN BEHIND THE FRONT SHADE, IN HEAVIER
FABRIC. THE FABRIC HAD TO BE JOINED TO MAKE
UP THE NECESSARY WIDTH: THE VERTICAL SEAMS
ARE INCORPORATED INTO THE DESIGN.

BOTTOM A ROMAN SHADE MADE FROM THE SAME
FABRIC AS THE WALL COVERING BLENDS INTO THIS
ROOM DOMINATED BY COUNTRY CHINTZES.

RICH GOLDS AND REDS, IN TWO CONTRASTINGLY
TEXTURED FABRICS, COMBINE IN THIS BORDERED
SINGLE SCOOP ROMAN SHADE, WHOSE CORDING
METHOD IS SHOWN IN THE TOP DIAGRAM ON THIS
PAGE. PLEATS HAVE BEEN ADDED AT TOP AND
BOTTOM FOR EXTRA FULLNESS.

SINGLE-SCOOP ROMAN SHADE
*This is a Roman shade with extra fullness at the
base, in the manner of a festoon shade (see page
162). Pulling the cord causes the fabric to scoop, as
shown in the bottom diagram. The rings are set in 2
inches (5cm) from the side and, at the bottom, the
same distance up from the hem. They are 12 inches
(30cm) apart vertically. The cord is tied to one of the
lowest rings and threaded through the rest of the rings
as shown.*

SINGLE-SCOOP ROMAN SHADES

These shades (illustrated in detail on page 163) resemble true Roman shades in appearance and method of construction. They fill the window space with a flat piece of fabric. However, they have some fullness at the base, like festoon shades. An extra half a yard (50cm) or so of fabric is caught and secured by the cording (in the manner of festoon shades), so that when the shade is let down the base retains its "scooped" fullness. Translucent fabrics are particularly suitable for this style, especially when combined with curtains.

AUSTRIAN AND BALLOON SHADES

Austrian and balloon shades are often confused. Both types have fullness in the width. A balloon shade falls like a curtain to end in a series of deep, ruched scallops along its base: these take up the fullness in length – a surplus of about half a yard (50cm). An Austrian shade differs from this in having the fullness distributed along its entire length. The fabric required for an Austrian shade amounts to twice the length of the finished drop and is gathered on cords inserted within the fabric during the construction of the shade.

Both shades operate in the same way as a Roman shade, with rings attached to the back of the shade through which cords, secured to the lowest ring, are threaded. A timber lath, covered separately, is fixed to the window frame by screws or brackets. This will house the screw eyes for the pulley cords to thread through, as well as support the shade itself. At the back of the shade's heading, Velcro tape is fixed: this joins to a reciprocal strip fastened to the edge of the covered lath.

Both Austrian and balloon shades, and particularly the Austrian, can tend toward complexity. This aspect can be used positively – perhaps to counteract a plain curtain hung simply at the window. On the whole, however, it is a characteristic that needs to be played down. Plain fabrics will display the form of these shades to best effect, and prevent too complicated a composition. Heavily patterned fabrics will fail: the pattern will be greatly diminished in all the ruching, and the general impression will be one of excess.

In a balloon shade, the number of scoops or scallops across the bottom can vary according to the design. The amount of fullness across the

◁

THIS TAILED BALLOON SHADE HAS BEEN MADE FOLLOWING THE CONSTRUCTION PRINCIPLES ILLUSTRATED AND DESCRIBED BELOW. THE SYMMETRY OF THE TAILS IS STRENGTHENED BY THE TALL TABLE LAMPS.

▷

AN UNUSUAL SHADE IN LACE, STRUCTURED LIKE A BALLOON SHADE BUT WITHOUT THE TRADITIONAL PENCIL-PLEAT FULLNESS ACROSS THE WIDTH. INSTEAD, MINIMAL FULLNESS IS CREATED BY PLEATS.

A TAILED BALLOON SHADE

The three diagrams below show the basic construction of a tailed balloon shade – essentially the same as an orthodox balloon shade, but with the cording omitted at the outside edges so that the two outer swags form tails instead of the usual rounded shape. The rings should be 12 inches (30cm) apart, and the lowest rings should be 2 inches (5cm) from the base of the fabric. The third diagram is a view from the front, showing the pencil-pleated heading, which is fixed to the timber lath by Velcro tape. The photograph (left) shows an example of this type of shade, with a roller shade behind.

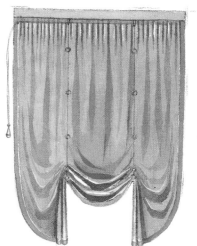

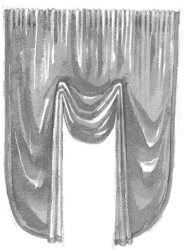

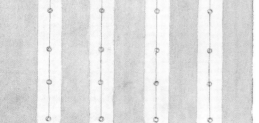

△

BALLOON SHADES IN VOILE FABRIC ARE SET WITHIN A LOOSELY DRAPED BUT FORMALLY SET SWAG AND CURTAIN ARRANGEMENTS. THE BALLOON SHADE COULD STAY ALMOST PERMANENTLY COVERING THE WINDOW, AS A SUN SHIELD.

◁

INVERTED PLEATS ALONG THE CONTRAST COLOR OF A VERTICAL PRINT GIVE A CERTAIN DEGREE OF FULLNESS TO THIS SHADE WITHOUT APPEARING EXCESSIVE.

A PLEATED BALLOON SHADE

This type of shade (illustrated in the diagrams, left) is characterized by pleating at the top which opens out down the length of the fabric. The basic construction of the pleats is shown in the two upper diagrams, before and after sewing: the join should be about 2 inches (5cm) or more, depending on the precise effect wanted. The cording of the finished shade, through rings sewn onto the back of the pleats, is shown in the lower diagram (back view).

width (2½×) remains unaltered regardless of the number of scoops you have. However, the number of scoops does affect the degree of ruching. For example, a shade with one large scoop will have relatively shallow ruching, whereas a design with several narrow scoops will be more emphatically ruched. The number of scoops might be chosen to relate to the window panes.

The bottom of a balloon shade can be ornamented with a frill, but it is best to avoid frills taken up the sides. Plainer borders, though, can work well: either vertical inset lines running down the shade at calculated intervals, or just around the edges. A narrow border running along the heading edge is particularly effective on a plain fabric.

Austrian shades are often at their best in one of the more translucent fabrics, such as muslin or plain cotton, to give a quieter, lighter effect. When they are hung with curtains, the overall look is rather formal.

TAILED BALLOON SHADES

These blinds are constructed in the same way as ordinary balloon shades, but with the cording altered to give a magnificent tailing effect. The "tails" are formed from what would otherwise be the outer swags/scoops of the shade, the omission of the cording at the outside edge causing the fabric to fall into an interesting tailed shape. Tailed balloon shades can be made with as many scoops as you wish between the tails, but a single, central scoop is usually the most effective choice.

PLEATED BALLOON SHADES

Balloon shades may have pleating, formed at the top of the shade and opening out as the fabric falls. Usually, this type of shade has only one or two scoops at its base, whereas the standard balloon shade tends to have more.

The fullness across the width is minimal, because the heading is generally straight except where the pleats occur. This gives you the option of using rather more figurative patterning. The surplus length, pulled up and secured with the cording so that the shade when down holds the fullness in the scoops, is best left fairly modest. The pleating may be of two kinds: inverted, or kick, pleats, closely spaced; or box pleats, spread at intervals.

THE FABRICS ILLUSTRATED ON THE FOLLOWING
PAGES HAVE BEEN PRECISELY IDENTIFIED WHERE
POSSIBLE. ADDRESSES AND PHONE NUMBERS OF
SUPPLIERS ARE GIVEN ON PAGE 179.

△

ACKERMANN'S *REPOSITORY*, IN THE EARLY 19TH
CENTURY, WAS A PERIODICAL PUBLICATION THAT
INCLUDED THE LATEST FABRIC DESIGNS. TODAY'S
COLOR MAGAZINES AND FABRIC AND DESIGN
DIRECTORIES SERVE A SIMILAR PURPOSE.

▷

THE MIXTURE OF PATTERNED FABRICS WITH PLAIN
IS OFTEN A SUCCESSFUL STRATEGY. HERE,
PATTERNED ROMAN SHADES AND PLAIN ROLLER
SHADES AGAINST THE WINDOW COMBINE IN A
QUIETLY ELEGANT ROOM.

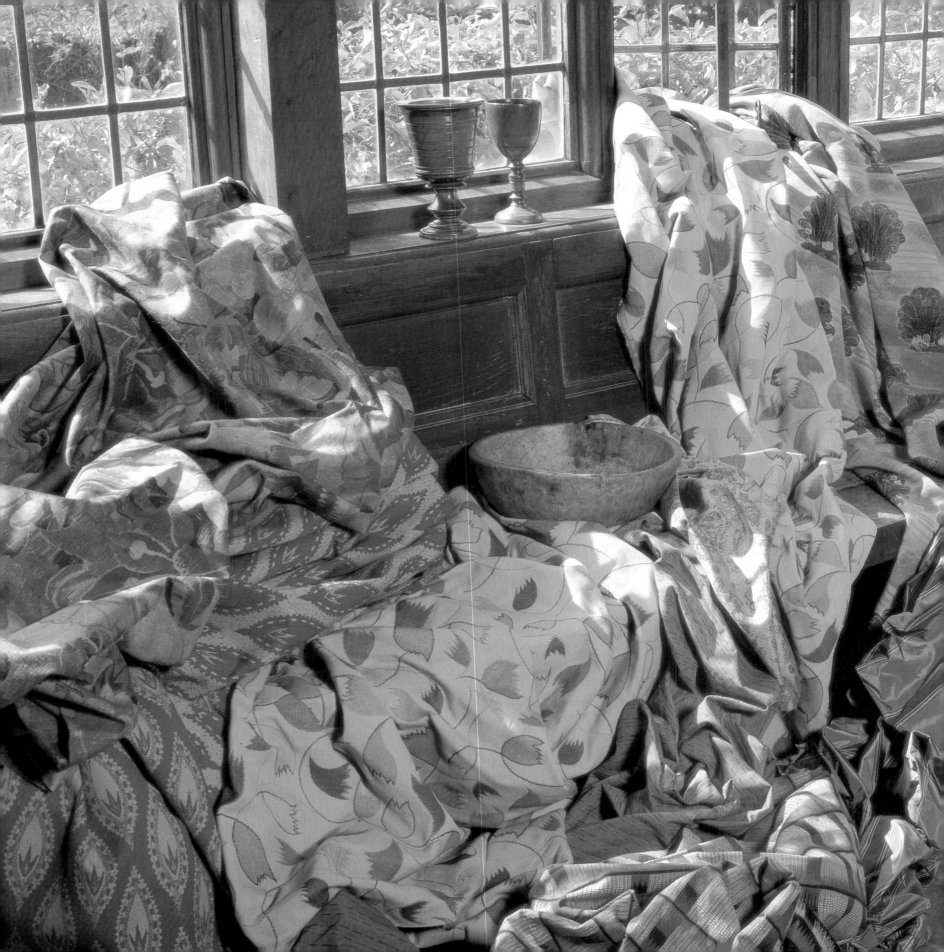

RICH PATTERNS

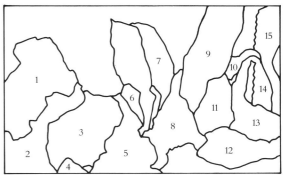

1 Cotton. Mathern col 1, J. Brooke Fairbairn
2 Cotton. Cypress FCY 04, Osborne & Little
3 Mainly cotton, some viscose. Carolina 12467, Sahco Hesslein
4 Cotton. Zadig 14357, Marvic
5 Mainly cotton, some viscose. Ariano 12499, Sahco Hesslein
6 Printed silk
7 Hand-painted silk. Bentley & Spens
8 Silk taffeta. Duse RS 66834, H.A. Percheron (Rubello)
9 Cotton. Allegro ST12 12, lined with Scarlatti ST1221, Pallu & Lake
10 Mainly cotton, some viscose. Marengo 12577, Sahco Hesslein
11 Cotton. My Lady's Garden M556278, Parkertex
12 Mainly cotton, some viscose. Madison 12521, Sahco Hesslein
13, 14 Cotton. Tabriz 14359, Marvic
15 Densely woven cotton, Rocroi, T110, Osborne & Little (UK)

All these fabrics are richly patterned, with a
range of glorious colors – gold and auburn for
tapestried weaves, through cool but shimmering
taffeta. Close tones in a sophisticated pattern (12)
create textural subtlety, while classic stripes (8) in
vibrantly contrasting colors are flatter, but still
ornate. Grandness is the unifying theme – but
not opulence. Patterns could be mixed, or used
singly for drama.

The hand-painted silk (7), emblematic in gold
and black, could be striking as an unlined curtain
across an archway – both sides would then be
visible. Richly textured, densely woven cloths
like 5 or 15 would be suitable for heavy
four-poster bed curtains, where insulation and
esthetic appeal are equally demanded.

PALE TONES

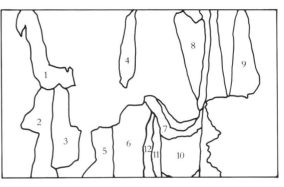

1 Chinese silk noil. MacCulloch & Wallis (not necessarily available)
2 Cotton. Line 31 6008, Mary Fox Linton
3 Twill weave. Shepton U2773–82, Parkertex (UK)
4 Cotton. Kim stripe col 10, Osborne & Little (UK)
5 Cotton/viscose. Jab International
6 Cotton/linen. Little Animals no 40, Celia Birtwell
7 Chinese Tussah twill silk (natural), MacCulloch & Wallis
8 Cotton. String 01 (Tamesa Weavers Collection), Osborne & Little
9 Cotton. Georgian stripe, Warners
10 Cotton lace. Nottingham Lace, Warners
11 Cotton. Matelas col 1, Création Baumann
12 Cotton. Arras M1359–90, Parkertex (UK)

Here are beautiful, changing tones, ideal when the intention is to create a mood of subtlety. From the delicately worked open weave of cotton lace (10) to the striped twill weave of the heavy cotton/linen mix (3), all these fabrics are understated, but nonetheless stunning in their fineness. Good backdrops for these fabrics would be terra cotta tiles, or polished wood floors – environments with their own distinguished texture.

Overprinting a darker shade – say, beige or taupe – on cream (6 and 4) creates an interesting textural effect, although the fabric is essentially flat. Use pale colors in abundance. Natural silk always drapes well and, whether its surface is mat (1) or shiny (7), will catch the light.

FLORAL PRINTS AND CHINTZES

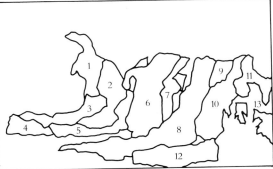

1 Glazed cotton print. Coromandel JF 701, Interior Selection
2 Cotton print. Longford 2026/05, Colefax & Fowler (UK)
3 Toile. Buckingham Toile 8763, Pallu & Lake (Charles Hammond) (available from Lee Joffa)
4 Glazed cotton. Spencer-Churchill (UK)
5 Printed cotton. Leaf and Bird LB3, Hill & Knowles
6 Glazed cotton. Fiorita F104–01, Designers Guild
7 Glazed cotton. Striato F106–01, Designers Guild (UK)
8 Printed cotton. Oviedo 05, Osborne & Little (UK)
9 *Toile de Jouys,* H.A. Percheron
10 Glazed cotton. Wild Orchid RF 703–01, Muriel Short (Titley & Marr)
11 *Toile de Jouys,* H.A. Percheron
12 Printed cotton. Judith 01, Osborne & Little (UK)
13 Linen. Les Vases 1485, H. A. Percheron

With the exception of the *toile de Jouys* fabrics (9 and 11), these printed cottons in joyful colors all take inspiration from flowers and foliage. Floral patterns need careful selection. In a room that is richly furnished, it might be preferable to choose muted colors and patterns that are not too dense. The easiest on the eye here would probably be 1 and 8: these have a traditional feel, in contrast to the vibrant, contemporary style of those in the middle of the group (6 and 7).

Different printing methods will produce varying effects. The *toile de Jouys* motifs are etched on copper plate, whereas the patterns on the other fabrics are screen- or roller-printed.

Textures

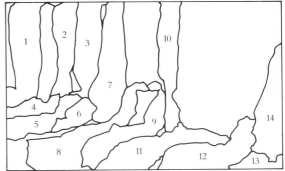

1 Woven cotton
2 Woven cotton/viscose. Striped Misa Moiré 4331–15, Marvic
3 Traditional damask. La Salle Ribbon Damas T839–15, Warners
4 Woven cotton. Promenade F4107–02, Designers Guild
5 Woven cotton. Sunstitch FWS-24, Osborne & Little (UK)
6 Linen. Blue on grey, Karl's
7 Woven cotton. Safi 09, Osborne & Little
8 Traditional damask. Laroma damask T835/7, Warners
9 Woven cotton. Sunstitch FWS-11, Osborne & Little (UK)
10 Woven cotton. Palace Dot (both sides), Daphne Tyson Fabrics
11 Woven cotton/viscose. Striped Misa Moiré 4330–11, Marvic
12 Woven cotton/viscose. Tulipan 4453–16, Marvic
13 Woven cotton/viscose. Aries 3869–6, Marvic
14 Woven cotton. Kerman M1361–93, Parkertex

Fabrics woven from the same fiber can look very
different from each other – thanks to variations
in the weaving techniques and in the texture of
the yarn. The distinguishing characteristics of the
woven fabrics shown here are the minimal use of
color, combined with strong pattern, raised to
give a rich textural quality.

The traditional damasks (3 and 8) need to be
carefully displayed so that their large, clear
patterns are seen to full effect. In contrast, the
smaller patterns – regimented, stylized flowers
(12) or richly colored geometrics (4 and 7) –
almost positively benefit from being twisted and
wound.

Patterned woven fabrics can look interesting
on the reverse, as in 10. A combination of both
sides in one item – for example, a bordered
curtain – can be particularly successful.

GRAPHICS

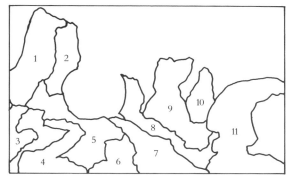

1 Cotton. Quadro 11–6064, Mary Fox Linton
2 Cotton. Classic 11–5733, Mary Fox Linton
3 Cotton, satin finish. Timney-Fowler
4 Animal Trellis no. 9, Celia Birtwell
5 Cotton. Omega Fi95E, Osborne & Little
6 *Toile de Jouys,* H. A. Percheron
7 Cotton discharge print. TF47, Timney-Fowler
8 Cotton. Reputation
9 Cotton. Timney-Fowler
10 Cotton. Little Animals p, Celia Birtwell
11 Cotton. Salome 01, Osborne & Little (UK)

Black and white prints make for striking
contrasts. Even twisted and gathered up, the
graphic patterning is not necessarily diminished.
The fine lines on fabrics 6 and 9 here create
beautiful images redolent of pen-and-ink
drawings. Compare the very dense mat black of
7 with the changing density of black in 1,
overprinted with its silver grid. A houndstooth
check in black and white receives two different
treatments here – in 2 and 3.

While mostly modern designs, these graphics
do not necessarily demand modern settings.
Some have a classicism that would suit a formal
period room.

Black and white prints can work well in
combination, but you could also try a
juxtaposition with a bright color – perhaps
flashes of red or gold to emphasize the
monochrome starkness.

BRAIDS AND TRIMMINGS

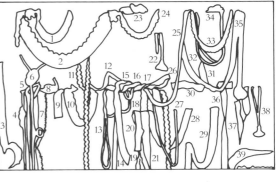

1, 3, 15, 20, 24, 29, 30, 31, 33, 35, 36 Tissunique
2 Fan-edged fringe. G. J. Turner
4, 6, 13 Cords and rope. Tissunique
5, 7, 17 Osborne & Little
8, 19, 22, 38 Key tassels. Daphne Tyson
9, 18, 28, 37 Houlès
10 Red and white fringe. Daphne Tyson
11 Gimp braid. Houlès
12 Dark red rope. Laura Ashley
14, 16 Two-tone fan edging. Colefax & Fowler
21, 27 Picot braid. Colefax & Fowler
22, 38 Key tassel. Daphne Tyson
23 Heavy ropes. Daphne Tyson
25 Black and white ropes. Daphne Tyson
26 Picot braid. Osborne & Little
32 Blue Carlisle cord: Henry Newbery. Red braid: Houlès
34 Rope. Daphne Tyson
39 Rope bullion. Osborne & Little

Braids and trimmings are reappearing in a major
way in many of today's curtain arrangements.
There is a wide range of styles to choose from,
and some wonderfully rich color combinations.
Traditional items such as picot braids (with
patterns of small loops), gimp, fan-edged fringes
and the like are available, but for some of the
natural fabrics currently popular it might be
more appropriate to choose plain cotton.

Flat braids (9 and 26) can be applied to curtain
edges, set in some distance to form a strong
visual border. Along the base edge of valances,
they can look equally eye-catching.

Braids and trimmings can create an interesting
textural surface, contrasting with lustrous silk or
taffeta or with a mat surface such as muslin or silk
noil. Silky edgings (such as 3, 24, and 29) catch
the light.

Fringing (2, 28, 10) should be hung so that the
fringed part hangs away from a curtain or valance
edge. Rope cord can be sewn into the edge of
thick interlined curtains, or used to border the
hemming of a valance. Rope is used for goblet
pleat headings, as well as tie-backs.

GLOSSARY

À la duchesse A type of bed with a canopy suspended from the ceiling, rather than supported by posts. Also known as an angel bed.

Architrave A wooden surround to a door or window frame. Also, the molding around an arch.

Austrian shade A shade that is ruched down the whole of its length, so that billows are formed when the shade is raised.

Box pleats Flat, symmetrical pleats formed by folding the fabric to the back at each side of the pleat.

Brocade A rich fabric with an embossed design, originally in gold or silver. The term has come to mean any flowered fabric with a raised pattern.

Brocatelle A BROCADE-like fabric, usually of silk or wool.

Buckram A sized coarse cotton or linen used as stiffening.

Café rod A slim rod, usually of brass, used for CASED or SCALLOP-HEADED curtains.

Cased heading (or rod-pocket heading) A curtain heading consisting of a simple, hemmed top through which a rod or narrow pole may be slotted.

Cheesecloth A loosely woven cotton cloth.

Chintz A cotton fabric, usually glazed, printed in colorful patterns of flowers, fruit and birds. The term was originally applied to painted muslin imported from India.

Clerestory window A window set high in a wall, usually above a sloping roof.

Cornice A shaped, stiffened drapery across the top of a window, used ornamentally and to hide the curtain rod. Also, a decorative molding at the top of a wall, just below the ceiling.

Cornice board A horizontal board used to support a CORNICE and sometimes as a base for swags and tails.

Cornice pole A curtain pole with rings, used for heavy curtains.

Dacron A synthetic fiber used for filling and padding.

Damask A silk or linen fabric with a textural pattern woven into it. The pattern is reversed on the "wrong side" of the fabric.

Dormer window A window that projects from a sloping roof.

Fascia A rectangular board, set vertically to cover a curtain heading or shade fixtures.

Finial An attachment placed at each end of a curtain pole, originally to stop the rings falling off, but usually treated as a decorative addition.

Flemish heading A GOBLET HEADING in which the pleats are linked along their base by hand-sewn cord.

French pleats (or pinch pleats) On a curtain heading, hand-sewn triple pleats separated by flat areas.

Goblet heading A curtain heading consisting of hand-sewn tubes whose tops are stuffed with PADDING or contrast fabric.

Half-canopy A rectangular canopy above a bed, extending only part-way down the bed from the headboard.

Interlining Soft material sewn between a curtain and its lining to add bulk, to improve the "hang" of the curtain, and to improve insulation.

Inverted pleat (or kick pleat) A pleat formed like a BOX PLEAT in reverse, so that the edges of the pleat meet in the middle on the right side of the fabric.

Knife pleats Sharply pressed, narrow, closely spaced pleats, all running in the same direction.

Lambrequin A stiff, shaped surround to a window. Unlike a CORNICE, a lambrequin continues down the sides of the frame.

Lining A secondary hanging sewn in at the back of a curtain to protect it from the light and improve its hanging qualities and insulation.

Moiré Watered silk or a synthetic substitute thereof.

Moreen A wool or wool-and-cotton mix heavyweight fabric, usually with a watered pattern.

Muslin A fine, gauzy cotton.

Padded edge A rolled fabric border, stuffed to make a "sausage" shape.

Padding A soft, bulky material for stuffing and packing out shapes, as in GOBLET HEADINGS.

Palladian window (or Venetian window) A window with a high, round-topped central section and two lower, square-topped side sections.

Pencil pleat heading A curtain heading formed by a tape which, when drawn up, creates a row of narrow, densely packed folds.

Pinch pleats see French pleats.

Piping Fabric-covered cording used to emphasize the edge of a curtain, CORNICE or TIE-BACK, often let in at a seam.

Polonnaise A bed set lengthwise against the wall and surmounted by a small dome.

Repp A fabric with a ribbed appearance.

Return The part of a curtain, cornice or valance that turns around the sides.

Reveals The sides of a window opening, at right angles to the faces of the wall and the window itself.

Rod A plastic or metal fixture from which curtains are suspended when a pole is not used. Modern rods often have cording systems and overlap arms. Some curtain rods can have a VALANCE rod clipped onto them.

Double rods are also available, for use with two layers of fabric.

Roller shade A shade operated by a spring mechanism so that when let up it coils itself around the cylinder in which the mechanism is located.

Roman shade A corded shade with horizontally set rods at the back, causing the shade to form a series of lateral pleats when raised.

Scalloped heading A heading with deep, rounded cut-outs, which slots onto a rod or pole.

Smocked heading A heading of pencil pleats anchored together at regular intervals to create a honeycomb effect.

Swag A generous scoop of fabric hanging from two fixed points over a window or bed.

Taffeta A thin, almost transparent fabric of woven silk.

Tails Hanging trails of fabric, either shaped and stiffened or falling fluidly from the ends of swags.

Tape-gathered heading A curtain heading formed by a narrow, threaded tape sewn on at the top of the curtain. When the parallel threads are pulled up, a gathered effect is created.

Tie-back A shaped and stiffened band, tasseled cord, sash or ribbon used to hold back curtains.

Toile de Jouys A fabric, originating in France, with pictorial scenes printed in one color (usually a deep pink) onto a cream background.

Turkish bed A narrow bed set into a draped recess.

Valance A soft fabric skirt that hangs from the top of a window or bed, as an alternative to a CORNICE.

Venetian window see Palladian window.

Voile A finely woven, semi-transparent cotton or silk fabric.

Worsted A woollen fabric made from twisted yarn.

The addresses below include suppliers of the materials illustrated on pages 167–177.

FABRICS

Laura Ashley Inc.,
714 Madison Avenue,
New York, NY 10021
(800) 367 2000

Bentley & Spens (hand-painted silks and cottons),
Studio 25, 90 Lots Road,
London SW10
(01) 352 5685

Bernards Designer Fabrics
P.O. Box 1063,
Independence, KS 67301
and
P.O. Box 23,
Peapack, NJ 07977
(800) 433 0863
Discounted designer fabrics

Celia Birtwell
distributed by
Gregory Evans,
509 North Robertson
Boulevard,
Los Angeles 90048
(213) 275 9040

Colefax & Fowler
distributed by
Clarence House Imports,
211 East 58th Street,
New York, NY 10022
(212) 752 2890

Conrans
Citicorp Center,
160 E. 54th Street,
New York, NY 10022
(212) 371 2225

Création Baumann
distributed by
Carnegie,
110 North Center Avenue,
Rockville Center,
New York, NY 11570
(516) 678 6770

Designers Guild
distributed by
Osborne & Little,
Suite 1503N, 15th Floor,
D & D Building,
979 3rd Avenue,
New York, NY 10022
(212) 751 3333

Greeff Fabrics
Designers Signature,.
200 Garden City Plaza, Garden
City,
New York, NY 11530
(516) 741 9440

Hill & Knowles
distributed by
Clarence House Imports,
211 East 58th Street,
New York, NY 10022
(212) 752 2890

Interior Selection
distributed by
S.M. Hexter,
27800 Superior Avenue,
Cleveland 44114, Ohio
(216) 969 0146

Jab International
distributed by
Stroheim & Romann Inc.,
155 East 56th Street,
New York, NY 10022
(212) 691 0700

Liberty of London
229 E. 60th Street,
New York, NY 10022
(212) 888 1057

Mary Fox Linton
distributed by
Intair C.P.S. Design Inc.,
180 N.E. 39th Street,
Miami, Florida 33137
(305) 573 8956

MacCulloch & Wallis
25 Dering Street,
London W1
(01) 629 0311

Marimekko
7 W. 56th Street,
New York, NY 10019
(212) 581 9616

Marvic
distributed by
Clarence House Imports Ltd,
111 8th Avenue,
Base 807,
New York, NY 10011
(212) 752 2890

Osborne & Little
distributed by
Clarence House,
101 8th Avenue, Room 801,
New York, NY 10011
(212) 752 2890

Paine & Co.
49–51 Barnsbury Street,
London N1 1TP
(01) 607 1176

Pallu & Lake
distributed by
Lee Joffa,
800 Central Boulevard,
Carlstadt, New Jersey 07072
(201) 438 8444
and
Stroheim Romann,
31–11 Tomson Avenue,
Long Island City,
New York, NY 11101
(718) 706 7000
and
Art Lee Fabric,
100 New South Road,
Hicksville,
New York, NY 11801
(516) 681 9340

and
Duralee,
1175 5th Avenue,
Bayshore,
New York, NY 11706
(516) 273 8800

**Parkertex & Baker Fabrics
Ltd**
distributed by
Old World Weavers,
979 3rd Avenue,
New York, NY 10022
(212) 355 7186

H. A. Percheron
97–99 Cleveland Street,
London W4P 5PN
(01) 580 5156

Reputation
186 Kensington Park Road,
London W11
(01) 580 7641/2

Sacho Hesslein
distributed by
Bergamo Fabrics,
3720 34th Street,
Long Island City,
New York, NY 11101
(718) 392 5000

Arthur Sanderson & Sons
979 Third Avenue, Suite 403,
New York, NY 10022
(212) 319 7220

Muriel Short
distributed by
Ken Jones Marketing Services,
11A Spa Creek Landing,
Annapolis, MD 21403
(301) 267 8552

Timney-Fowler Ltd
distributed by
Christopher Hyland,
Design and Decorating
Building,
979 3rd Avenue,
New York, NY 10022

Daphne Tyson Fabrics
261 Main Street,
Dennisport, MA 02639
(617) 394 2146

Warner & Sons Ltd
distributed by
Greeff Fabrics Inc.,
155 East 56th Street,
New York, NY 10022
(212) 888 5050
and
E. C. Carter Inc.,
The E. C. Carter Division of
Greeff Fabrics Inc.,
155 East 56th Street,
New York, NY 10022
(212) 888 5050

TRIMMINGS

J. Brooke Fairbairn
distributed by
Boussac of France Inc.,
Decorating and Design
Building,
979 Third Avenue,
New York, NY 10022
(212) 421 0534

Houlès USA
8584 Melrose Avenue,
West Hollywood,
Los Angeles
(213) 6526171

Henry Newbery & Co. Ltd
distributed by
Lee Jofa,
800 Central Boulevard,
Carlstadt, New Jersey 07072
(201) 438 8444

Standard Trimming Co.
306 E. 61st Street,
New York, NY 10021
(212) 755 3034

Tissunique Ltd
distributed by
Rist Corp.,
Design Center,
300D Street SW, Suite 338/40,
Washington DC 20024
(202) 646 1540
and
Classic Revivals Inc.,
1 Design Center Place,
Suite 545,
Boston, MA 02210
(617) 574 9030

G.J. Turner & Co. Ltd
23 Phipp Street,
London EC2A 4ND
(01) 739 5037

Thanks are due to all the designers whose arrangements appear in the photographs in this book, and in particular to:
Monika Apponyi (pp 59L/C, 76, 93, 98, 119L, 140BR, front cover)
Ashley, Laura (p 129TR, photo reproduced courtesy of Weidenfeld & Nicolson)   Bill Bennette (p 129BR, 132TR, 143C)
Lars Bolander (half-title, pp 96, 149L)
Tom Britt (p 64TL, 141BC)   Boudin (142, 143TL)
Nina Cambell (pp 34, 46R, 47, 49 (with Lady Vestey), 60, 79L. 104. 110TL (with Lady Vestey), 112BL, 136R, 147R, 151TR)
Colour Counsellers (pp 81R, 114T, 139)
Cooper & Perkins (pp 48R, 147L)   Colleen Covington (p 57)
CVP design (pp 30T, 32, 106TR, 146TCL)
Hannele Dehn (pp 37, 53L, 80TL, 102R)
Sissi Edmiston (pp 24, 71, 77, 91, 113TR)
Dido Farrell and Charmian Hawley (pp 62TL, 97, 108L, 115, 125, 127, 132L)   Anna Fendi (p 82)
Vincent Foucard (pp 19, 62BL, 86-7, 87T/B, 99L, 110BL)
John Fowler (p 14B)   Derek Frost (pp 161R, 163CL)
Christophe Gollut (pp 21, 42TL, 64B, 66, 72-3, 144, 163TL, 165)
Mark Hampton (pp 74, 78L, 100, 141TL, 148L)
David Hicks (pp 41L, 113BR, 148R, 159)
Kelly Hoppen and Charlotte Barnes (pp 2-3, 4, 36, 72L, 90)
Conrad Jameson (pp 22R, 23, 110BR, 112-13, 123, 132TC, 151CR)
Pru Lane-Fox (pp 67, 75, 84-5, 103L, 118L, 141TR)
Mary Fox Linton (pp 50, 53R, 160C)   Meryl Marshall (p85R)
Marvic (pp 27R, 48L, 94T)   Meltons (p 106BL)
Fee Michael (p 163R)   David Mlinaric (pp15L, 41R, 65BR, 80R)
Andrea de Montal (pp 21, 95, 106BR, 112TR)
Richard Mudditt (p 73R)   Louise Murray (pp 42R, 43, 68-9)
Fernanda Niven (p 78R)   Mimi O'Connell (pp 38R, 39, 51L, 62BR, 92L, 114C, 121, 145 156C/CT)
Melanie Paine (pp 57, 70, 89, 94, 116, 124, 155TL/B, 161L)
Graham Rust (pp 59R, 157L)   John Saladino (pp 99R)
David Shilling (p 35)
John Stefanidis (pp 154, 162T)   Alexandra Stoddart (pp 61CB, 146TCR)   Michael Szell (p 6)
Barbara Thornhill (pp 25L, 29, 33, 66C, 68-9, 68TR, 106TL, 107L, 133TR, 156B)
Top Layer (pp 27L, 65L, 64R, 92R)   Valentino (pp 82, 101)
Victoria Waymouth (pp 26, 63T, 66R, 103R, 117, 119R, 133TL/TC)

Melanie Paine designed the pennanted and scooped muslin four-poster valances on page 115. With Jacqui Small, she also styled the photographs in the Materials Directory (pp 166-77).

Many thanks are also due to all those who kindly allowed photography in their homes, and especially to: Peter Afia, Laura Ashley, Charles Beresford-Clark, George Cooper, Colline Covington, Christophe Gollut, Jenny Grey, Erzherzog von Hapsburg, Charmian Hawley, Mrs Haresh, Bob Lawrence, Valerie Louthan, Mrs Patinio, Philip Sayer, Suki Schellenberg, Mrs Shearer, Jacqui Small, Graf Spreti, Mrs Steevens, Mary Stewart-Hunter, Michael Szell, Lady Katherine Vestey, Lady Waymouth.

Grateful acknowledgement also to the following historic houses whose guardians allowed photography.
Ebenezer Alden House, Union, Maine (pp 44, 45, photos reproduced courtesy of British *House and Garden* © The Condé Nast Publications Ltd)
Fota, Co. Cork (p 16, photo reproduced courtesy of *The World of Interiors*)   Ham House, Osterley (p 12BL)
Leeds Castle, Kent (pp 8, 9, 10, 62, 142, 143BR, 153) (note that the bedroom on p 9 is not open to the public)   Luttrellstown (p 11C, 68L)
Marble House, Newport, Rhode Island (p 13T, photograph reproduced courtesy of British *House and Garden* © The Condé Nast Publications Ltd)
Nostell Priory (pp 11L, 13CT/CB/B, 15L/R)
Old Battersea House, Battersea (pp 46R, 81L)   Stretton Hall (p 14B)

The authors and publishers would like to extend their gratitude to Raymond O'Shea of the O'Shea Galleries, London, for supplying all the historic archive pictures that appear in this book.

VELCRO ® is a trademark in the USA, owned by Velcro USA Inc.

INDEX